Walking in on Mum and Dad

Walking in on Mum and Dad
Adventures in Embarrassment

BRIAN KING

Icon Books

Published in the UK in 2007 by
Icon Books Ltd, The Old Dairy,
Brook Road, Thriplow,
Cambridge SG8 7RG
email: info@iconbooks.co.uk
www.iconbooks.co.uk

Reprinted 2007

Sold in the UK, Europe, South Africa and Asia
by Faber & Faber Ltd, 3 Queen Square,
London WC1N 3AU
or their agents

Distributed in the UK, Europe, South Africa and Asia
by TBS Ltd, TBS Distribution Centre, Colchester Road
Frating Green, Colchester CO7 7DW

This edition published in Australia in 2007
by Allen & Unwin Pty Ltd,
PO Box 8500, 83 Alexander Street,
Crows Nest, NSW 2065

Distributed in Canada by
Penguin Books Canada,
90 Eglinton Avenue East, Suite 700,
Toronto, Ontario M4P 2YE

ISBN-10: 1-84046-805-X
ISBN-13: 978-1840468-05-2

Typesetting by Hands Fotoset

Printed and bound in the UK by Creative Print and Design

CONTENTS

ABOUT THE AUTHOR

Brian King is an award-winning pioneer of radio fly-on-the-wall documentaries, the producer of hundreds of programmes for BBC Radio 4, including the long-running series *On the Ropes*, and, with Martin Plimmer, the co-author of the best-selling *Beyond Coincidence* (Icon, 2004). His latest book is *The Lying Ape* (Icon, 2006).

DEDICATION

To Ben and Dan, with apologies for any embarrassment I may have caused you.

ACKNOWLEDGEMENTS

Thanks first to Andrew Furlow, Marketing Director at Icon Books, without whom this book might never have been written. Andrew had emailed me a proposed design for the cover of my last book, *The Lying Ape: An Honest Guide to a World of Deception*. I didn't much like the look of it and, believing it to have come from an outside company, wrote back saying: 'Don't these people have any imagination at all?' Back came his reply: 'Actually, it was my idea.' I apologised profusely, explaining that I was always putting my foot in it and that, in fact, my whole life had been one long series of embarrassing moments. 'There's probably a book in it', I suggested, '*Oh Mein Faux Pas*'. Andrew replied: 'I think there might be a book in it … but not sure about the title.'

And here it is, complete with much better title, courtesy of Icon director Simon Flynn, to whom many thanks. Thanks also to my admirably ruthless editor Duncan Heath.

Much gratitude is also due to psychologist Robert Edelmann, whose excellent books and papers on the subject of embarrassment were a major inspiration, and to the many friends, relatives and complete strangers whose humiliating but highly entertaining misadventures are exposed here.

I have occasionally changed names to protect careers, reputations and marriages, but mostly the victims are exposed in all their red-faced mortification.

CHAPTER ONE

THE CURSE OF EMBARRASSMENT

This book will, I fear, cause me considerable embarrassment.

It seems only fair that, if I'm to expose the daft and embarrassing things done by others, I should also reveal my own, depressingly long catalogue of humiliating blunders and misadventures.

I am the man who, as I believe this book cover discloses, was chased, terrified, from a BBC department meeting – by a moth. Not, I confess, the only occasion on which lepidoptera have conspired to make me look stupid. *Embarrassed by Moths* would have made an equally fitting title for this book.

I am also the sixteen-year-old who passed out on the first day of his new Saturday job at his local supermarket.

Employed to serve on the delicatessen counter, I spent the first couple of hours of my first shift watching colleagues slice ham, weigh olives and shovel assorted salads into plastic tubs. Nothing to it. Eventually I was invited to serve my first customer, a fussy individual who wanted half a dozen slices of bacon, *just so* thick. I hoisted the meat onto the electric bacon-slicer, fitting the safety cover as instructed, and proceeded to slice. *Too thick*, said the man. I adjusted accordingly. *Too thin*, said the man. Somehow in the process of turning my attention backwards and forwards between customer and bacon-slicer, I managed to bring the tip of the middle finger of my right hand into contact with the machine's spinning blade. A cold sensation, a quick withdrawal of hand … a whole lot of blood.

I stared for a while at my fingertip, trying to establish how much had been removed, or indeed, remained. But there was … so much blood. Feeling dizzy, I reached out to retain my balance, slumped against a pair of scales and sent the brass weights flying off in all directions. Then, like Philip Marlowe slipped a Mickey Finn, my world dissolved.

A fuzzy-edged version of the delicatessen manager approached me. I collapsed into his arms and passed out. Regaining consciousness briefly, I found myself bouncing on the manager's shoulder as he strode through the store; customers were nudging each other and pointing at me. I slipped back into blessed oblivion.

I finally regained consciousness in the staff kitchen, being offered a cup of strong sweet tea. Brenda, the canteen manager, was wrapping yards of gauze around my finger which had, in reality, suffered nothing more than a nick to the fleshy tip. But there had been … so much blood.

A lesser teenager might have called it a day, but I was determined to get straight back on the bacon-slicer. Which I did. The tiny scar on my right-hand middle finger has long since faded. The memory of its cause is as vivid as ever.

Moths and supermarket bloodbaths are just the tip of a very large iceberg of embarrassment in my life. Other highlights involve broom cupboards, short-sightedness, feigned death and at least one further bout of unconsciousness. We'll come to those later.

I have never, however, experienced the particular horror of walking in on Mum or Dad in flagrante delicto – nor for that

2

matter, of being walked in on by my children, though I don't doubt it's very traumatic for all concerned.

US singer Janet Jackson walked in on her parents when she was a small child. Confused and troubled by what she had seen, she had to have it explained to her by her older brother Michael. Who better to put you straight on the subject of sex?

* * *

Embarrassment, as you are probably all too painfully aware, lurks around every corner and under every stone.

There is embarrassment in failure and in success, in being wrong and in being right.

There is embarrassment in forgetfulness, in stupidity, in weakness, in carelessness, in slips of the tongue, in being early, in being late, in being in the spotlight, in being left out in the cold. There is embarrassment in poverty and in wealth.

There is embarrassment in spilling, tripping, dropping, incontinence, nudity, phobia, flatulence, drunkenness, injury, illness, karaoke, trainers, mobile phones and sex. There is embarrassment in fruit – particularly the banana.

Embarrassment is everywhere.

> At a reception held shortly before Charles de Gaulle's retirement, his wife, Yvonne, was asked by Harold Macmillan's wife, Dorothy, what she most looked forward to in the coming years. 'A penis', declared Mrs de Gaulle without hesitation. An embarrassed silence was broken by the President, who came to his wife's rescue, explaining: 'My dear, I think the English pronounce it 'appiness ...'

As this widely reported, but sadly almost certainly apocryphal story demonstrates, embarrassment can be very amusing, at least from a distance. But it's also a curse.

Acute embarrassment is never more than a faux pas away. You might return from a visit to a restaurant toilet with soft, pink tissue paper stuck to your foot, or lock yourself out of your house in your Rupert Bear pyjamas, or forget the name of the special guest you are introducing to an audience, or be caught in mid-rant against your mean-spirited, ungrateful, lying, deceitful, bully of a boss by the sudden blinding revelation that he's standing right behind you.

Photographer Chris Shaw published an anthology of pictures he took during the 1990s while working as a porter in various hotels in London, Paris and New York. The book – *Life as a Night Porter* – includes several curious shots of a naked man padding along a hotel corridor. He had got out of bed to go to the toilet, still rather the worse for drink, stepped into the corridor by mistake and closed the door behind him. According to Chris, this sort of thing would happen two or three times a week, and it was his unenviable and all-round-embarrassing task to let them back into their rooms.

Embarrassment strikes indiscriminately. It's no respecter of ability, wealth or status. It does tend to favour the inebriated, though its full impact in such cases is generally postponed until the morning after. In its mildest form, embarrassment causes little more than slight discomfort; a more-or-less benign force teaching us to be more circumspect in future about what we say and do. But at the other end of the scale it can become a hugely negative and destructive emotion, often causing us far greater distress than our actions deserve.

Embarrassment makes us feel like fools. It makes us want the earth to open up and swallow us whole, makes us want to shout: 'I CAN'T BELIEVE I JUST DID THAT!' Embarrassment can ruin careers. Embarrassment, as we shall see, can kill.

And embarrassment is embarrassing.

Actress and singer Carol Channing would invite her nightclub audience to ask her personal questions. 'Do you remember the most embarrassing moment you ever had?' someone asked one night. 'Yes, I do!' Channing replied. 'Next question?'

Not everyone, thank heavens, is so unforthcoming.

Here are tales of sex and seduction gone horribly wrong, of indecent exposure on a grand scale, of emails which should never have been sent, of goalkeepers throwing the ball into their own net, of infidelity revealed (by a parrot), of erections in a nudist colony, of wedding speeches which provoke brides to reach for the cake knife. Here are stories of heads of state fleeing from killer rabbits, or accidentally extinguishing the eternal flame. Here is embarrassment at work, rest and play.

These mortifying memoirs have been gathered from friends, family, colleagues and from a wide variety of other sources. *Guardian* columnist Zoe Williams, for example, offered these insights into her personal world of embarrassment ...

One time I sneezed on some bald fella's head while I was walking down the street, and his wife told me off.

Another time, I dropped 50p into a guy's turn-up on a really crowded tube, and I had to get it back off him because I needed it for the bus fare, so I had to rootle about round his ankle.

I had this one-night stand once, and I left in the guy's trainers, because they were the exact same colour and shape as mine (grey suede Pumas), only four sizes too big. I don't know what I was thinking, I just figured maybe I'd lost some weight off my feet. Overnight.

It's not, I think, in Zoe's nature to be overly disconcerted by such minor misadventures, but not everyone is as resilient to the mortifying power of embarrassment.

> Founding member of The Goons, Michael Bentine, was at a theatrical audition, listening to a woman singing on stage. 'Her voice was so awful that I turned to the man sitting beside me and remarked upon it', recalled Bentine. The man replied frostily: 'That's my wife.' Pink with confusion, Bentine hastily stammered: 'I didn't mean her voice was awful, only the song she was singing.' To which the man replied: 'I wrote it.' Bentine slunk away.

Embarrassment, even over the most trivial of things, can haunt its victims for ever. A friend told me the following rather charming story about something which happened to him more than twenty years ago, but asked me not to use his real name. It is still, incredibly, a source of some considerable shame for him. He suggested I call him John Kennedy, so I will.

The wrong side of the duvet

When John Kennedy went away to university, his Mum bought him a duvet. Coming from an Irish working-class family, he'd grown up with sheets, blankets, and the odd overcoat on the bed, so the duvet was a bit of a puzzle. He ended up climbing into it and doing the poppers up so only his head stuck out.

All was fine until a girlfriend, wise in the ways of modern bedding, called to visit and found him still in his duck-down cocoon.

He's a wiser man now, though.

The ubiquitous nature of embarrassment is reflected in our newspapers. The press gorges on embarrassment, revelling in the humiliation, or assumed humiliation, of its victims. On Tuesday, 25 July 2006, a day like any other, countless millions of people will have said, done or observed something which will have caused them embarrassment. Millions more will have chosen not to do something for fear of embarrassment. On this particular day the newspapers reported, amid their usual diet of war and Su Doku, three distinctly sorry tales.

A stiff sentence

US Judge Donald D. Thompson was convicted by a jury in Oklahoma on four counts of indecent exposure. He had been surreptitiously masturbating, using a mechanical 'penis pump', while presiding over trials in Creek County Court.

His former court reporter, Lisa Foster, wiped away tears as she gave evidence that during one of the trials, she heard the pump's distinctive 'sh-sh' sound.

One newspaper report of the case observed that the 59-year-old district judge had not chosen the most appropriate moment to 'take the law into his own hands'.

Some embarrassment can be brushed aside, excused, explained, forgotten or forgiven. My guess is that Judge Thompson may struggle to recover his judicial gravitas – once he has come out of prison, that is.

Online love

Love-struck Joseph Dobbie will long regret his decision to pour out his heart in an email.

His electronic missive was sent to Kate Winsall, a girl he had met at a party, asking her to meet him for coffee. It waxed lyrical about how he had decided to 'listen to my heart' and how her smile was 'the freshest of my special memories'.

Which would have been fine if Kate's sister hadn't got hold of the email and forwarded it to all her friends. And even that might not have mattered if all her friends hadn't decided to follow suit, generating a chain reaction which sent the email into millions of homes around the world, turning Joe Dobbie's emotional outpourings into a huge internet joke.

Joe had promised to keep the memory of Kate's smile 'for moments when I need to find a smile of my own'. Such a moment had arrived.

A clearly embarrassed Joe later conceded that his chances of getting a date with Ms Winsall were now desperately slim.

Unlike Judge Thompson, Joe will probably fully recover from his experience. He may be a little more cautious in future about his use of the internet, but he will live to love again.

Two in the bush

Pop star George Michael was spotted emerging from bushes on Hampstead Heath in north London, follow-ing 'a sexual encounter with a pot-bellied, jobless van driver'. George's long-term partner Kenny Goss was reported to be outraged and threatening to call off their planned 'marriage'.

George Michael refused to admit he had been embarrassed by

the media exposure of his shenanigans. He was not, so to speak, going to give the press the pleasure. Far from being crushed by the revelations, he responded by saying that his latest escapade wouldn't jeopardise his planned marriage, that he saw nothing to apologise for in his behaviour. 'A very large part of the male population, gay or straight, totally understands the idea of anonymous and no-strings sex', he explained. At least he wasn't using a penis pump.

These three tales of misadventure were all reported on the same day, but open any newspaper, any day, and you will find their like.

* * *

Embarrassing situations, like dog turds, are hard to avoid, however careful we may be. Even the most self-assured, rich and powerful will, from time to time, put their foot heavily and squelchily in it.

> A state banquet during a tour of Japan back in January 1992 shouldn't have presented too many problems for US President George Bush. He had aides to advise him about the subtleties of oriental etiquette. But things still went terribly awry.
>
> Halfway through the meal, Mr Bush turned to his host, Prime Minister Kiichi Miyazawa, and in flagrant disregard of protocol, vomited copiously into his lap. He then slumped dramatically under the table.
>
> The President reappeared a few moments later announcing that he felt 'great'.

Slumping under the table was an interesting demonstration of the innate human instinct to hide from embarrassment. President Bush's son, George W., has had his fair share of hide-under-the-table moments, and he too has had trouble with food, once spectacularly forgetting to chew before swallowing a pretzel, causing him to choke and fall to the floor, suffering cuts and bruises to his face. It was maliciously rumoured that CIA officers were subsequently employed to pre-chew his food. Not to mention (though, of course, I will later) his ongoing struggle with the English language.

Not many of us will ever have the opportunity to vomit in a prime minister's lap, however much we might want to. But anyone might be delayed en route to a concert hall.

> The American pianist and comedian, Oscar Levant, had begun his New York performance of a piece by Poulenc when a woman, arriving late, attempted to take her seat. The mischievous Levant promptly stopped playing and glared at her. The woman paused briefly, then took a few tentative steps forward, which Levant immediately accompanied on the piano. Diddly-dum. Diddly-dum. The woman stopped again. Levant stopped. The woman took a few more quick steps forward, imitated by Levant on the keyboard. Diddly-dee. Diddly-dee. The woman stumbled on, Levant musically mimicking her movements as in a silent movie soundtrack. The audience roared with laughter as the woman, red-faced and on the verge of tears, eventually made it to her seat.

The former England football manager, Sir Bobby Robson, was once asked what he might have done if he hadn't gone into sport. His response: 'I'd have given my right arm to be a concert pianist.' Many more embarrassing slips of the tongue, including the greatest hits of George W., to come.

* * *

Troublesome as embarrassment can be, I am not suggesting that society would necessarily be a better place without it. Sociologist Erving Goffman observed more than 50 years ago that embarrassment serves an essential social function, acting as a subtle and pervasive constraint upon brash and insensitive behaviour. He argued that:

> Too little perceptiveness, too little savoir-faire, too little pride and considerateness, and the person ceases to be someone who can be trusted to take a hint about himself or give a hint that will save others embarrassment.

Some people clearly do behave as if oblivious or indifferent to the consequences of their words and deeds. Other, more perceptive, proud and considerate souls, are all too easily embarrassed. This book, I hope, will help identify a third way; a way to keep such things in proportion, a way to live a life less mortified without alienating all those around us.

If fear of embarrassment plagues and controls our lives, then only by better understanding this most curious of human emotions can we escape from its icy grip and live our lives free of dread.

Amid the welter of distress and misery contained in these pages are seeds of hope; the hint of a cure or antidote to the shame and unhappiness we pile upon ourselves. Answers lie in learning from others' mistakes, in caring less, in wholeheartedly embracing humiliation and, surprisingly, from tap-dancing.

This book will help you fight the curse of embarrassment, and spare your blushes, enabling you to lead a better, more fulfilled life, free of the fear of further mortification. It will also, I suspect, give you a damned good laugh at the expense of the many hundreds of people whose stories of red-faced misadventure are mercilessly (and unashamedly) exposed here. But never forget; there but for the grace of God …

This book is not an entirely comprehensive digest of embarrassment. Such a book would be immensely long and difficult to lift. I didn't have room for accounts of vegetarians being served steaming plates of pig's offal at dinner parties, or surgeons sawing off the wrong leg, or firemen getting stuck in trees while trying to rescue cats. Such things happen, of course, but will have to be taken as read.

But there's plenty here to compensate. This modest attempt to cover the waterfront offers a disturbingly revealing insight into the menace that is embarrassment and will serve you well in your daily struggle to avoid its thrashing tentacles.

CHAPTER TWO

THE ROOTS OF EMBARRASSMENT

Man is the only animal that blushes ... or needs to.

Mark Twain

Embarrassment is a natural part of being human. It springs from our fundamental need to belong, emerging when we accidentally step out of line, or believe we have, or fear we will. If we could control our instinctive, knee-jerk reaction to embarrassment it might not be such a problem for us. The trouble is, we can't.

Too often we are guilty of what sociologists refer to as 'emotional deviance' in our response to embarrassment, reacting in ways that 'differ in quality or degree' from what is expected in given situations. We convince ourselves that we have fallen further from social grace than is actually the case. A small faux pas, a failure to keep an appointment or a minor slip of the tongue can haunt us for a lifetime. Leaving a single fly button unfastened transforms into a case of gross indecent exposure, likely to bring the vice squad knocking at the door.

We have become super-sensitive to embarrassment. Stars of stage and screen have no immunity – often quite the reverse.

Beam me up

While staying in a hotel one evening, Shakespearian actor Patrick Stewart – best known for his role as Captain Jean-Luc Picard in *Star Trek: The Next Generation* – ordered room service and turned on the TV. While channel-surfing, he stumbled upon an episode of *Next Generation* which he barely remembered having filmed, and settled down to watch. 'I had forgotten that I had ordered room service', he recalled. 'The man arrived with my order. He looked at the television, and ... looked at me ... with such pity ...'

Why would Patrick Stewart find this situation embarrassing enough to still haunt him many years after the event? Why do any of us experience this strange and powerful emotion? Does it exist simply to ensure that we operate within the rules of polite society, or does it have some deeper primeval function?

We begin our journey of discovery by travelling deep inside the brain, following a case history reported in 1982 by New York neurologist Professor Orrin Devinsky.

Devinsky observed how George, a 38-year-old doctor, had been in apparently excellent health when he suffered a sudden brain seizure ... a grand mal. A year later, George began to experience the first of many episodes of what he described as 'the feeling of extreme embarrassment, as though I had made a very foolish remark'. The episodes occurred at social gatherings, during consultations with patients and while alone. The odd thing was that none of them were related to any behaviour which could remotely be described as 'embarrassing'.

Surgical investigations revealed an explanation – a tumour deep within the medial aspect of the right frontal lobe of

George's brain. Electrical discharges in both frontal lobes appeared to be producing the sensation. Here then, it seemed, was where the emotion of embarrassment was located.

Prof Devinsky's revelation is supported by evidence presented by medical patients with personality disorders caused by frontal lobe brain damage. In some cases such damage results in unprompted embarrassment, in others it produces an almost total inability to be embarrassed, as uncomfortably observed by psychologist Cordelia Fine in her book *A Mind of Its Own*.

> While doing my PhD I studied a man who had damaged part of his prefrontal cortex in a car accident. Because he had a little problem with his temper (he liked to let an iron bar do his arguing for him), for the safety of all he had been removed to a high-security psychiatric hospital. I made the mistake of reading his case notes just before meeting him and I felt deeply nervous as to how the two of us would hit it off. Unfortunately when I am anxious my palms become unpleasantly sweaty. As I began to shake hands with the patient, he rapidly withdrew his own with an expression of the utmost disgust, and ostentatiously wiped it on his trousers. 'Christ!' he remarked to my supervisor. 'It's like shaking hands with a wet haddock.' Had his prefrontal cortex been intact and doing its job, I have no doubt that he would have kept his observation to himself.

So our capacity to feel embarrassed nestles in our frontal lobes. OK. But why is it there and what, in evolutionary terms, is its purpose?

A very short history of embarrassment

It's widely held that we are the only animal that feels embarrassment, but we can't know this for certain. When we observe the body language displayed by a cat which falls awkwardly or the puppy that has chewed its master's slippers, it does look as if they are embarrassed – the hangdog/cat expression. But maybe not. Appearances, animal behaviourists insist, can be deceptive.

Going purely on empirical evidence, we must conclude that embarrassment is a uniquely human trait. But when did it begin? Did prehistoric man blush with embarrassment if he arrived for the mammoth hunt, having left behind his spear? Did prehistoric woman hide her face in shame if she turned up at a cave-warming in last year's fur?

Good questions, to which, alas, I have no good answers. Certainly we know that embarrassment was alive and kicking in Ancient Greece. Plato tells us, for example, of how his great philosopher friend Socrates was embarrassed by becoming lustfully aroused by a glimpse beneath the robes of his (Plato's) uncle, the Athenian statesman Charmides.

We can reasonably assume that wherever and whenever social rules were introduced, embarrassment rapidly followed. Embarrassment, in a sense, is the price we pay for civilisation, for becoming *cultured*. But the emotion probably didn't get into full swing until the publication of the early papyrus editions of *Debrett's Etiquette and Modern Manners*.

The Victorians hid their sexual voraciousness behind a smokescreen of prudery, setting themselves up perfectly for embarrassment.

The Bishop and his wife

The 19th-century British admiral Lord Charles Beresford was in love with Lady Warwick, who also happened, by the by, to be the apple of the Prince of Wales' eye at the time. On this particular occasion, Lord Beresford and Lady Warwick had been invited to a house party, and that night he tiptoed into her darkened room.

Closing the door quietly behind him, he jumped onto the bed shouting 'Cock-a-doodle-doo!', only to find himself between the Bishop of Chester and his wife.

Such was the extent of Lord Beresford's embarrassment, he felt it necessary to leave the house the following morning without taking breakfast.

Biographer Anita Leslie can vouch for this story, because it was told to her grandfather by Lord Charles Beresford himself. And how many *Carry On* films and Whitehall farces did it inspire in the next century?

Psychologists studying Eskimo communities in the 1970s observed that some still practised an ancient ritual in which embarrassment was applied to teach children to avoid natural dangers. If a child were to fall through thin ice and survive the experience, the rest of the village would gather round and point and laugh at the shivering victim. The theory was that fear of further embarrassment was a greater deterrent to skating on thin ice than the prospect of a bone-chilling dip in sub-zero water.

Embarrassment has been used extensively down the centuries as a means of controlling criminal and other anti-social behaviour. Petty thieves in medieval times would be placed in a pillory or stocks and pelted with rotten fruit. In 12th-century London, bawds and 'whore-mongers' had their heads shaved and were led to the pillory by minstrels, while subjected to ritual abuse from the crowd. Other felons might be made to ride backwards on a horse and crowned with a fool's cap. And one priest, discovered in flagrante delicto, was paraded through the streets with his breeches down around his ankles.

Modern versions of this approach to punishment persist to this day. In 2003, Shawn Gementera pleaded guilty before a San Francisco court to stealing letters from local mailboxes. As part of his sentence he was required to spend a day standing outside a local post office wearing a sandwich board stating: 'I stole mail; this is my punishment.'

The fashion for 'shaming punishments' began in the early 1990s in the US and has grown rapidly in popularity.

- Judges in the states of Arkansas and Wisconsin, Maryland, Texas, Georgia and California have ordered shoplifters to parade in front of the stores they have robbed, carrying placards proclaiming their guilt.
- In Ohio and Illinois, drunken drivers have been issued special licence plates that identify them to fellow motorists.
- In Pittsfield, Illinois, a farmer had to display a sign outside his driveway declaring: 'Warning. A Violent Felon Lives Here. Travel at your own risk.'
- In Houston, Texas, a man who pleaded guilty to domestic violence was ordered to stand on the steps of City Hall and apologise to passers-by for hitting his estranged wife.
- And my favourite … A court in Cleveland, Ohio, after hearing that 44-year-old Stephen H. Thompson had made obscene hand gestures and shouted 'pigs' at local police officers, ordered that he should stand on a street corner next to a 350-pound pig with a sign that read: 'This is not a police officer.'

And shaming punishments are not unknown in Britain.

In November 2002, police in Brentwood, Essex, introduced a poster campaign identifying criminals sentenced to more than a year in jail. Their names, pictures, crimes and sentences were displayed in local restaurants and train stations. And in 2003, authorities on the Isle of Wight came up with a cunning plan to reduce violent behaviour among children on school buses. Offenders were made to travel to and from school in a bright pink 'bus of shame', effectively branding them as delinquents. In a rather neat extra touch, the heating was taken out of the bus to make the journey even more uncomfortable.

More recently, the Channel 5 show *Swag* found a way of adapting the concept into a form of entertainment – embarrassing miscreants with exposure on national television. They staged a series of stunts aimed at encouraging thieves to exhibit their larcenous natures in front of hidden cameras.

This could be considered entrapment, but it's hard not to cheer out loud as would-be felons snatch unattended bicycles which promptly belch thick, bilious smoke, or steal cars which fill up with foam. In another set-up, a lorry's tailgate is left open, revealing a tempting cache of booty. A man clambers inside, the doors slam shut and the canvas sides of the lorry fall away to reveal that he's trapped in a cage. As the lorry moves off with its reluctant passenger, the driver shouts through a loudhailer to passers-by that he has a thief in the back.

How embarrassing – to appear on a television network with such low viewing figures.

* * *

We may not be absolutely sure when the emotion of embarrassment first developed, but we can be fairly sure it's here to stay.

Our technological age has created infinite opportunities for embarrassment. Television and radio broadcast our faux pas to vast audiences as quickly as we can commit them. Email and other forms of electronic messaging enable us to communicate more quickly than we can engage our brains, with inevitable consequences. All of which we will consider in future chapters.

We now replace our mobile phones every five minutes to avoid being embarrassed by an old model, but these brain-frying contraptions offer a wide range of pitfalls. Who has not, from time to time, responded enthusiastically to a jaunty 'How are you?' or 'Would you like to come round to my place for a bit of hanky panky?', only to discover that it's not you that is being addressed, but the mouthpiece of a Nokia 8800?

The Director of the BBC Proms, Nicholas Kenyon, was being interviewed live on Radio 4 about conductor Sir Simon Rattle's decision to restart a concert because it had been disrupted by a member of the audience's mobile phone. Kenyon's attempt to comment was rudely interrupted by the insistent ring tone of a mobile phone. It was his own. And I, having instructed an audience at the recording of a radio debate to switch off their phones, was mortified when the proceedings were immediately interrupted by the strains of the *Monty Python* theme squawking from my own mobile.

The future isn't so much orange, as red – red with embarrassment.

Red-faced blues

Whether or not we are unique in our capacity to be embarrassed is debatable, but Mark Twain's observation that man is the only animal that blushes would appear to be accurate. Other species do change skin colour for camouflage, but there's no evidence that the giant octopus or chameleon are reacting to some aquatic or lizardly gaffe.

Blushing is basically a rather unfortunate side-product of our instinctive 'fight or flight' response to situations we perceive as threatening. Like what? Like the time I was innocently sitting in the audience of *Mother Goose* at the Birmingham Hippodrome and my five-year-old son stood up and identified me as the 'mummy or daddy who is singing out of tune'. In my book, being hauled out of an audience by Cilla Black to sing in front of hundreds of strangers counts as a threatening situation. Though not generally prone to such a reaction, I blushed.

In the event I was spared total humiliation by the timely intervention of another small boy sitting a couple of rows in front, who had simultaneously pointed to his own father. God bless him. But why had I blushed? I blushed because my nervous system had been over-activated – increasing my heart rate, pumping blood to my face, neck and chest. My brain had sensed danger and was preparing me for fight or flight. The problem was, as is invariably the case in embarrassing situations, there was no one to fight and no option for flight. And, of course, blushing itself makes things worse, feeding the sense of embarrassment.

But blushing is just one of the many physical signs of embarrassment. We draw attention to our discomfort in a variety of ways: fidgeting with our hair or clothes, turning away, closing our eyes, stammering, stopping the world and getting off. Closing our eyes, according to Freud, is our way of denying an experience. In relation to embarrassment, we instinctively lean towards the ostrich option, like George Bush Snr sliding under the table. If we can't see them, they can't see us – and we needn't be embarrassed.

Displays of embarrassment and associated blushing are equivalent to an appeasement gesture in other animal species; rolling over and playing dead when attacked. In other words, they serve the function, socially, of saying: *You are the superior one, now leave me alone.*

This sounds right. Most of us are familiar with the desire to avoid becoming too much the centre of attention. Why, otherwise, is it so uncomfortable for us when friends and relations sing 'Happy Birthday'? The tuneless assault on the senses is surely not the entire story.

Herd instinct, the need to remain safe and anonymous within the group, seems a more likely explanation. Stepping outside of the protective crowd singles us out for attention by predators. The lion watches the herd, looking for the straggler, the weak or clumsy individual who has 'eat me' written all over him. We are all prospective carrion. Invited to a dinner party, I arrive to discover that it's a posh champagne and caviar affair. I am wearing jeans and carrying a bottle of Blue Nun. The lion strikes.

The psychology of embarrassment

I'm ashamed of how easily I get embarrassed. Or do I mean I'm embarrassed by how easily I get ashamed? Shame tends to be about feelings of guilt, whereas embarrassment is more about inadequacy and incompetence. And embarrassment involves being observed, or thinking we have been observed, doing something stupid, whereas shame can be experienced in miserable isolation. But to most intents and purposes we can treat the two emotions as more or less the same thing. Well I'm going to, anyway.

Most psychologists settle on something along the following lines for a definition of embarrassment.

Embarrassment results from a failure of self-presentation, resulting in perceived diminution of public esteem.

We have a powerful need to feel good about ourselves. Too

much self-esteem, of course, can turn us into insufferable ego-tists, but too little can leave us at the mercy of embarrassment. This might result in nothing worse than mild shyness, a reluctance to say 'boo' to passing geese. But at the other end of the spectrum, it can lead to social anxiety or even social phobia.

> *Social phobia – a persistent, irrational fear of, and compelling desire to avoid, situations in which the individual may be exposed to the scrutiny of others. The fear that we may behave in a way that will be humiliating or embarrassing.*

Social phobia can manifest itself in a variety of crippling conditions, such as acute introversion, performance anxiety (stage-fright) and agoraphobia, but it's all, fundamentally, about fear of embarrassment.

The experience of embarrassment is bad enough, but it's the prospect of such things happening, the *fear* of embarrassment, which is the more destructive force. Fear of making fools of ourselves can result in us making nothing of ourselves. Fear of embarrassment generates insecurity and destroys self-belief. When we say we don't have the confidence to do something, to sing or dance or tell a joke, perhaps at the heart of our anxiety is the fear that we will screw up and face the embarrassment of failure.

* * *

The extent to which we suffer or fear embarrassment varies throughout our lives. Tiny infants, for example, are immune, because they have not yet developed the self-awareness required to experience the emotion.

Experiments were carried out in the late 1980s to test when

self-awareness, and potential for embarrassment, kicks in. Toddlers ranging from twelve to 24 months old had little smudges of rouge placed on their noses, and were then deposited in front of mirrors. Up until the age of fifteen months, the babies didn't seem to recognise themselves as *themselves* in the mirror. By 24 months, every baby tried to touch or wipe his or her nose. They knew they were the baby reflected in the mirror, and had reached a new level of self-awareness.

Psychologists then tested the same children for embarrass-ability. They were profusely praised for being smart or cute, or for their lovely hair or beautiful clothes. They were asked to dance or sing in front of strangers. Only the children who had touched their noses, the children with self-awareness, showed any of the classic signs of embarrassment – blushed, or fidgeted or averted their eyes.

Our potential to be embarrassed increases as we grow older and become more self-conscious and begin to care more what other people think of us. By the time we reach adolescence, our capacity for embarrassment roars into overdrive. Confusion about our identity, sexuality and self-worth provides the ingredients for almost non-stop mortification.

As adults, at least in theory, we gain more control of our emotions, developing coping mechanisms to avoid embarrass-ment. In practice, many of us never completely lose our adolescent hang-ups and allow our lives to be inappropriately dictated by fear of appearing foolish. It's not until old age that we tend to stop caring what other people think of us and start behaving as we damn well please.

* * *

We have problems with seeking and accepting help, embar-rassed that it demonstrates weakness or presents a 'negative self-image'. Millions of pounds in social security benefit are unclaimed every year. Others fail to claim disability benefits, or refuse to accept support from social services.

Interesting psychological studies have been conducted into our curious attitudes to being helped. In one experiment, subjects were asked to solve a complex detective story, and were required to seek advice along the way. They could choose to be helped by either a physically attractive or physically unattractive person. Attractiveness was determined by proper scientific means (i.e. the subjective opinion of a dozen or so people), but you have to wonder if those involved were told by what criteria they were being selected. Anyway, it turned out that men sought less help from a physically attractive female than from a less attractive female, but that women consistently plumped for the more attractive male.

The experimenters concluded:

> For females, displaying dependency on a male is congruent with the feminine sex role: consequently a female's display of relative inferiority by help-seeking actually represents a positive presentation of the self. In this case therefore the helper's physical attractiveness facilitated rather than inhibited help-seeking behaviour. For males, asking females for help violates sex-role definitions of expected behaviour, and hence reflects a negative presentation of self, resulting in an increased possibility of embarrassment.

Confident, well-adjusted people will take advice from anyone, whether they look like Marilyn Monroe or Quasimodo, but what if they were required to seek help from a child?

In another experiment, subjects were set a spelling test in which they could choose to seek advice from either a child or adult of comparable spelling ability. Subjects most frequently chose the adult, feeling, according to the experimenters, that to accept help from a child would result in 'negative presentation of self' and cause embarrassment.

No one seems yet to have conducted an experiment evaluating our responses to seeking advice from attractive or non-attractive children. And how might we react to taking advice from small rodents or amphibians – male, female, attractive or otherwise? I have noticed that my neighbour's cat rarely asks my opinion about anything. I now realise this is because it finds it embarrassing to take advice from an inferior species. And does the potential embarrassment of association with inferior beings account for the fact that we never get visited by extraterrestrials? Someone should look into this.

* * *

Some people march through life behaving as they like, saying what they think and caring not a jot what impression they create; oblivious or indifferent to the consequences of their words and deeds. These are the *Unembarrassables*, people capable of laughing in the face of social death. In some instances it's the result of a clinical disorder.

Ros Blackburn was diagnosed as 'severely' autistic in infancy. Like many others with the condition, she has developed sophisticated techniques to overcome her lack of social communication skills, and now, in her thirties, travels the world addressing conferences about her condition.

One beneficial aspect of her autism, she says, is her inability to be embarrassed: 'I am quite relaxed in social situations because I don't get embarrassed', she explains. 'I don't get self-conscious. I couldn't give a monkey's what people think, therefore I'm not so worried about looking the part or acting the part or whatever, that I can't enjoy myself.' She is, however, rather curious about what embarrassment might feel like.

But the vast majority of Unembarrassables are not clinically autistic, nor, like Cordelia Fine's patient, brain-damaged. They just seem blind to the potentially embarrassing consequences of their actions. Their lack of inhibition can, however, land them in big trouble.

Le road rage

Laboratory technician Alain Basseux lost his temper when a motorist cut him up at a roundabout in Yorkshire. The Frenchman chased the offending car for two miles, forced the vehicle to the side of the road, yanked open the door and threatened to kill the driver if he drove so inconsiderately again. He then kicked shut the door.

Monsieur Basseux's lawyer told a court that his client was mortified when he discovered that his victim was a director of the company that employed him. He was less embarrassed apparently by his actual behaviour which, the court was informed, was commonplace in France.

A bit of me admires Monsieur Basseux's lack of restraint. I know I would have acted with far more circumspection. In fact, I know I wouldn't have acted at all.

I'm the kind of motorist, like you probably, who sits stationary and stewing in his car on the inside lane of the motorway, while other drivers blithely ignore signs instructing them to filter left, and roar by, forcing their way back into the queue just before the contraflow begins.

How can they do that? Don't they know that everybody hates them? Have they no conscience? No shame? If there was a God, surely he would make their cars break down a little further down the road. Or perhaps he could just make them a little more easily embarrassed, or me a little less.

What peculiar goings-on in the frontal lobes of our brains account for our differing attitudes to queue-jumping in general? Philosopher A.C. Grayling suggests that those who can, without apparent conscience, push in at the front of a queue are 'applying lashings of self-justification and rationalisation', convincing themselves that no one is harmed. The British seem generally less able to draw this conclusion than Americans, for example, and the very idea of queuing in the first place is anathema in many Latin countries. The British, by and large, will tolerate queuing, resisting the urge to queue-jump, but are too embarrassed to make a fuss if someone actually does. It results in a lot of silent seething.

* * *

Unembarrassables, in failing to pick up on the signals transmitted by others to stop whatever it is they are saying or doing, often create waves of embarrassment around them. They, of course, sail serenely through the storm. Such, I think, was the case with the woman who sat in the audience at the recording of an edition of the BBC Radio 4 programme *Heresy*, which I used to produce. Chaired by David Baddiel, a panel of broadcasters and comedians were invited to challenge the orthodoxy of various received opinions.

Up for discussion on this particular occasion was the widely held opinion that Christmas has become too commercialised. After an amusing debate, in which both David Baddiel and panellist Vicky Coren made much of their Jewish perspective on the issue, the audience was asked for its opinion.

DAVID BADDIEL: Are there any Christians in the audience? Don't be embarrassed.

[A WOMAN RAISES HER HAND]

DAVID BADDIEL: Madam. Do you feel, as a Christian, that Christmas has become too commercialised?

WOMAN: Yes it does get commercialised. But then it's strange because the people who are going to make all the money out of this are the Jews. And they don't believe. But they are doing all the selling.

[COLLECTIVE INTAKE OF BREATH BY AUDIENCE]

DAVID BADDIEL: Hang On. Excellent. How marvellous.

VICKY COREN: Wait a minute.

JOHN O'FARRELL [TO DAVID BADDIEL] And you killed Christ.

[RELIEVED LAUGHTER FROM AUDIENCE]

ARMANDO IANNUCCI: Next week *Any Questions* will be coming from Nuremberg.

VICKY COREN: Please, please, please. We must all stop while this mad woman says more. All the Jews do *what*?

WOMAN: It's strange that the people who profit most financially from this, are the people with all the shops.

VICKY COREN: And you think they are all Jews. Why do you think that?

WOMAN: We have always had influxes of immigration. At the turn of the century it was ... the Jews. They commercialised things.

VICKY COREN: Do you know there are only 300,000 Jews in Britain? How do you think they managed to get behind all the tills at Christmas? Do you think they travelled by sleigh?

WOMAN [LAUGHING]: I don't know ...

DAVID BADDIEL: It's interesting and unusual to have a dyed-in-the-wool, cast-iron racist on the show.
VICKY COREN: No, it's not racism … it's madness. She thinks there's a Jew in every shop.
DAVID BADDIEL: I think we should stop there. I have to go and find my yellow star.

The point about this exchange was that although the woman in the audience was being mercilessly ridiculed, at no point did she demonstrate the slightest sign of embarrassment. While her male companion squirmed in his seat, and the rest of the audience silently willed her to stop digging a hole, she careered on, blithely unaware she was saying anything untoward.

For most of us, such an experience would have felt like being put in the stocks and pelted with vegetables, This woman, I'm sure, will look back on the experience fondly.

* * *

Our capacity to mentally separate our actions from their consequences has been the subject of many academic studies down the years. Dr Stanley Milgram was the New York psychologist who, in the 1960s, conducted controversial experiments in which he encouraged participants to administer electric shocks to unseen victims who answered questions incorrectly. Milgram was trying to understand the mentality of the German concentration camp guards who justified their behaviour on the grounds that they were simply obeying orders.

Those taking part in the Milgram tests didn't know that their 'victims' were actors who were faking their reaction to the non-existent electric shocks. A worryingly large number were prepared to administer what they believed to be fatal doses of electricity if instructed to do so.

Milgram's conclusion was that his subjects had been prepared to hand over moral responsibility for their actions to figures of authority. But he observed that participants were also motivated by embarrassment. They didn't want to spoil the experiment or fail to perform as the nice men in white coats required. I'll be considering in a later chapter how our reluctance to report embarrassing symptoms to our doctor can lead to fatal consequences. Embarrassment can kill in more senses than one.

Years later, Milgram undertook another experiment which was slightly less dramatic, but more seated in common experience. In 1974 he took students down into the New York subway, shepherded them onto crowded trains and made them ask passengers to give up their seat. An astonishing 68 per cent of those approached willingly complied, preferring to stand rather than handle the embarrassing consequences of refusing a polite request.

Embarrassment is an immensely powerful emotion, capable of exerting considerable influence on our behaviour. In the following chapters we'll look at embarrassment in action, red in tooth and claw; and, attempting to avoid smirking, we'll try to work out as we go along where the victims went wrong, and how we might ensure we don't follow in their footsteps.

CHAPTER THREE

SEX AND SEXUALITY

Those of an easily embarrassed nature should consider skipping this chapter. I wish I had.

Brian King

We are, to the best of my knowledge, the only species on the planet that turns off the lights when it has sex. This most basic of human functions, and our sexual instincts and behaviour in general, have somehow become a source of great embarrassment to us.

Will Self's novel *Great Apes* imagines a world in which chimpanzees have become the dominant species. Sex on this version of Earth is unencumbered by social convention, anxiety and taboo, and is enjoyed openly and unselfconsciously on the street, in the office and at the supermarket. In the real world of human beings we are more inhibited about such things, tending to shun the horizontal Tesco tango.

How sweet it is

In a biology class at Harvard University, back in October 1998, a professor was talking about the high glucose levels found in semen. A young female student raised her hand and asked: 'You're saying there is as much glucose in male semen as in sugar?' The professor confirmed that this was correct and added some statistical data. Raising her hand again, the girl asked: 'Then why doesn't it taste sweet?' A moment of stunned silence and then the whole class exploded into laughter. Realising what she had inadvertently revealed, the embarrassed student snatched up her books and made for the door. As she retreated, the professor added: 'It doesn't taste sweet because the taste buds for sweetness are on the tip of your tongue and not the back of your throat.'

I can't absolutely guarantee the authenticity of this story, but it has been widely circulated on the internet, and Harvard University Medical School is a major centre for research into semen and fertility. Either way, it's easy to empathise with the young girl involved. We all, from time to time, reveal more about ourselves than we intend.

Back in the lecture theatre, circa 1920 ...

Ticket to ride

Oxford University lecturer Christopher Atkinson began a seminar by explaining that his observations about the life of Polynesian islanders would include details of their incredible sexual activities. Several female students, blushing with embarrassment, rose from their seats and made for the door.

'It's all right, ladies, you needn't hurry', Atkinson is reported to have called out. 'There's not another boat for a month.'

The great psychoanalyst Sigmund Freud wouldn't have been surprised by the students' discomfort. He believed that for all human beings, sexuality and anxiety are indivisible.

One challenge to the absolute truth of Freud's assertion came in the 1920s from American cultural anthropologist Margaret Mead, who claimed, four decades before the Swinging Sixties, to have found a society which experienced absolutely no feelings of sexual shame or embarrassment. She wrote in her book *Coming of Age in Samoa* that all the young women on the remote island of Ta'O appeared to enjoy casual premarital sex free of inhibitions or social constraints. I can't say if it was the same community Christopher Atkinson was talking about.

But in 1983, five years after Mead's death, the New Zealand anthropologist Derek Freeman published the results of a study which controversially questioned her findings. He argued that Mead's interviewees had been lying to her, and concluded that the South Sea Islanders were as sexually self-conscious and reserved as everyone else. Freud would have been nodding in agreement.

And we're barely less anxious and embarrassed about sex and sexuality when it's depicted in art.

Now you see it …

Among the many sculptures displayed by American art collector Peggy Guggenheim in the garden of her Venetian home was Marino Marini's spectacular 'Angel of the City', a bronze statue of horse and naked rider, in which the sculptor had attempted to capture the rider's ecstasy by casting him with an erect penis.

In deference to the delicate sensitivities of passers-by, including local nuns whose Holy Day processions went by Guggenheim's home, Marini had made the penis fully detachable.

How might the nuns have reacted if Peggy Guggenheim had overslept one morning and forgotten to unscrew the penis? Successive popes, residing just 350 miles south of Peggy's place, have displayed somewhat conservative attitudes towards sex, generally declaring it a functional rather than recreational activity. Indeed, most religions, officially anyway, see sex as more to do with procreation than pleasure, and this has doubtless contributed to our hang-ups about it.

Children inherit feelings of guilt and embarrassment about sex because their parents have such difficulty talking about it, shielding the little darlings from exposure to sexual images and language. Fielding simple questions such as 'Where do babies come from?', for example, can throw adults into a tailspin, reinforcing the impression that sex is a taboo and possibly dirty business. Telling our children that they'll go blind if they masturbate isn't enormously helpful either.

I flunked sex education. In fact I was almost old enough to grow a beard before I really got to grips with the subject, or indeed, a woman. My parents had been too embarrassed to explain anything to me, and it was nowhere to be seen in the school curriculum. I learnt a bit from playground chatter, which unfortunately led me to believe, for an absurdly long time, that girls got pregnant from kissing.

Whatever the psychological explanation, it's clear that we are inordinately embarrassed by sex: embarrassed about how to do it, how long to do it for, how to do it safely, how often to do it, and even where to do it.

I had promised myself that of all the embarrassing things that have happened to me, there was one incident I would never, under any circumstances, include in this book. But in the spirit of my argument that we should care a little less about what other people think of us, here goes.

We were young and drunk, but those are our only excuses. She and I were among a dozen or so college friends on a youth-hostelling weekend in Gloucestershire. We were staying in a converted Norman castle at St Briavels in the Forest of Dean.

After a night in the pub, passions inflamed and inhibitions suppressed in equal measure by alcohol, we staggered back to the hostel ahead of our friends and, insanely, made our way to the women's dormitory, shedding items of clothing as we went.

Somewhere at the back of my addled brain was the tiny thought that we might be interrupted by the return of other female youth hostellers, even members of our own party. I should have paid more attention to that thought. Moments later the door opened and in they came, decidedly unamused by our cavorting. The words 'disgusting pig' were bandied about, we were unceremoniously separated and I was pushed, semi-naked, from the room. Inebriation cocooned me from the worst of the humiliation at the time, but breakfast the following morning, consumed under disapproving glares from all quarters, was one of the most uncomfortable meals of my life.

And things got worse. Our whole company were subsequently banned for life from the Youth Hostel Association, not for sexual misbehaviour, but for failing to obey the strict 10.30pm curfew the following night. Setting off for the pub, we had delegated to one of our number the simple task of leaving a window open so we could creep back in after hours. When we returned at about midnight, we found the window, still ajar, but 70 feet up the sheer castle wall. We roused the camp oberfuhrer and explained that all our watches had mysteriously ceased to function during the evening, but he refused to let us in, and we spent a bitterly cold night shivering in bus shelters and telephone boxes. The problem with telephone boxes, incidentally, is that the light and the smell of urine tend to keep you awake.

Twenty years later I was driving through St Briavels with my wife and sons and decided to show them around the extraordinary 13th-century castle – still used as a youth hostel. We chatted to the current manager, and I was about to tell him about the miserable devil who had locked me and my friends out all those years ago, when a rare instinct for caution overcame me. Instead I asked him how long he had been in charge at St Briavels. Twenty-five years, he proudly informed us. Embarrassment, for once, was avoided.

Getting back to sex. My experience of being walked in on was, for me, a cause of excruciating embarrassment. Other people, however, are made of sterner, and indeed more ambitious stuff.

Three's company

Writer and broadcaster Michael Bywater was in bed with his girlfriend ... and her friend. This *ménage à trois* had been agreed following the consumption of large quantities of Worcestershire scrumpy. The action took place at the friend's family home, as Michael recalls:

> Things were going very satisfactorily – three is most certainly not a crowd, though it does present some logistical problems, but nothing insoluble with goodwill and the flexibility of youth – when the bedroom door opened and in wandered the inevitable dotty great-aunt. She gazed upon the scene for a moment and then said, unconvincingly: 'I was looking for the

lavatory.' She paused. Frozen into immobility, we paused too. 'Well', she said, 'this *is* nice. It's just like having your great-uncle Eddie back, but of course he died at the Somme … Night-night, dears.' And off she went again.

Michael had been too surprised by the great-aunt's appearance to attempt any defence of his compromising situation. Having some sort of explanation, however lame, can help.

Using your loaf

Samantha (not her real name, which is Sarah) had gone back to her boyfriend's house at 2am for a 'cup of coffee'. They were quite drunk (there's a bit of a pattern forming here) and decided to dispense with the caffeine and get straight down to sex, right there on the kitchen surface.

Suddenly her boyfriend's mother was standing in the doorway in her dressing gown. Samantha screamed and fell off the draining board. Her boyfriend, with remarkable presence of mind, snatched up a loaf of bread and announced that, despite considerable evidence to the contrary, they were 'just making a sandwich'.

Mollified, and mumbling something about thinking she was being burgled, his mother retreated. Somehow the moment was lost.

'Just making a sandwich' was of course how Michael Bywater should have explained away his *ménage à trois*, though the aunt would have probably spotted the absence of bread. But what on earth are you supposed to do if the dog's got it in for you?

Who let the dogs in?

One day Julie and her boyfriend were 'messing around' in her bedroom, while the rest of the family were watching television in the living room. All would have been fine if her dog hadn't taken it into its tiny canine head to snatch her carelessly discarded underwear, taking it downstairs to present to the rest of her family. Julie, on discovering the whereabouts of her lingerie, 'wanted to die'.

Before an audience

We generally prefer sex to be a private affair, undertaken behind closed doors and firmly pulled curtains, and with the volume held down low enough to avoid arousing the neighbours. Being heard having sex can be as embarrassing as being seen.

Oh baby

Bob and Doreen Cant had booked into a small hotel in Paignton in Devon, chosen because it advertised itself as 'child friendly' and provided a baby-listening service.

Explains Bob: 'A few nights into our stay, we decided to take advantage of this facility and after turning on the microphone one evening, we put the boys to bed and went for a drink at the local pub.'

Returning to the hotel, they found staff and guests milling around the reception desk listening to muffled oohs, ahhs and sighs emanating from a bank of speakers. They were eavesdropping on the amorous goings-on in various bedrooms, where the occupants had absent-mindedly forgotten to turn off their listening device.

'We shook our heads in disbelief', says Bob. 'How could anyone forget to turn their system off?'

Quite easily as it turned out. The couple retired to their room, raided the mini-bar, and after a few drinks, fell into amorous activity.

It wasn't until the morning, when they gave their room number at breakfast, and received a smirking 'And a very good morning to you', that it dawned on them what they had failed to do.

Actor and comedian Mat Horne's unintentional bedroom performance was limited to an audience of two – his parents.

I see a little silhouette …

It was a balmy summer's night and Mat was in his bedroom with his girlfriend. His parents were outside in the garden, sitting on a raised part of the garden which gave them a direct view into the room. Judiciously, Mat pulled the curtains and he and his girlfriend began to make love.

What they didn't realise was that the lamp beside the bed was throwing a perfect silhouette of their activity onto the curtains.

Later, after his girlfriend had gone home, Mat went into the garden to chat to his parents. How had their evening been? 'Very entertaining', they replied. Mat followed their gaze to his bedroom window, still clearly displaying the outline of the bed and crumpled sheets. 'It must have looked like a primitive outdoor blue movie', he said.

The matter was never spoken of again.

Trying to have unobserved sex can be particularly tricky for flat-dwellers.

Everybody needs good neighbours

Making love with his girlfriend one Saturday afternoon, Peregrine Andrews (not a pseudonym) looked up to meet the eyes of his septuagenarian neighbour. The doors to their flats were adjacent, and Peregrine's door, not properly closed, had blown open, leaving a direct line of sight into his bedroom.

'I was mortified', says Peregrine. 'I was worried he would think we were exhibitionists.' He considered confronting the matter head on, perhaps writing a letter, but it was all just too … embarrassing. When they next met, both behaved as if nothing had happened.

'Shortly after that he moved back to Canada and is now dead, though his wife still lives in the flat', says Peregrine. 'We talk a lot, but I have never asked her if her husband told her about what he saw that day. How could I?'

Being observed having pretend sex can be almost as embarrassing.

Plenty of room on top

While filming Ken Russell's version of *Lady Chatterley's Lover*, Sean Bean (Mellors) and Joely Richardson (Lady Chatterley) were required to cavort naked in a field. Don't worry, said a reassuring Russell, there's a ten-foot wall around us – no one will see. So Sean and Joely began to cavort, only to freeze in horror as a packed double-decker bus sailed past.

And then, of course, there are the people for whom public sex is not in the least bit embarrassing. This following incident was reported in the *Observer* newspaper.

Scoring at halftime

A couple were ejected from a Premiership football ground for having sex in the disabled toilet. Stewards were alerted when spectators complained that the door had been locked for half an hour and that the sounds emanating from inside did not suggest constipation was the problem.

The couple were completely unfazed by being apprehended, though the girl did have one request: 'My boyfriend is still in his seat watching the match', she explained, showing a steward her ticket number. 'Would you mind telling him you've thrown me out, otherwise he'll be wondering where I've gone.'

Which reminds me of the allegedly true story of the couple who had sex on a packed commuter train. Everyone just looked away and pretended it wasn't happening, and it was only when they had a post-coital cigarette that their fellow travellers rose to object. That's the British for you.

Even Mums and Dads do it

None of the exploits exposed so far come close to emulating the exquisite mortification of walking in on Mum and Dad, or being walked in on by your children. Getting people to talk about such experiences is not easy. Many who have been there have simply blotted the details from their memories; others are still in therapy and will discuss the experience only with their analyst.

So many thanks to those brave few who have agreed to spill the embarrassing beans.

> Karen Muntz, aged nine, rushed into her parents' room one morning to find her father energetically bouncing up and down on top of her mother. 'I didn't really have any idea what was going on', recalls Karen. 'But I'd never seen my father move so quickly.'

Karen's tender age and innocence protected her from any trauma. The incident, which occurred more than 40 years ago, was never discussed. When small children do the walking in, it's usually the parents who do the squirming, with the level of discomfort and mortification intensifying (and distributed more evenly) as the age of the child involved increases.

> A successful novelist, who prefers to remain anonymous, recalls how her son, aged ten, woke up one night and came into her bedroom as she and her husband were having sex. 'We stopped immediately and pretended nothing had happened', she says. 'We figured that he was so sleepy that if I just put him back to bed he'd think it was all a dream, and we'd get away with it.'
>
> But the next morning her precocious and observant son informed her: 'Mum, I think I know what you were doing. But I promise I won't tell anyone, and I'll do my best to forget it.'

Bless.

I have worked with author Bill Bryson on many occasions over the years, and found him to be a perfectly well-adjusted sort of chap. Certainly I've observed nothing to suggest he had been emotionally scarred by the childhood experience of wandering unannounced into his parents' bedroom, as recalled in his memoir *The Life and Times of the Thunderbolt Kid*.

> To my surprise, the shades were drawn and my parents were in bed wrestling under the sheets. More astonishing still, my mother was winning. My father was obviously in some distress. He was making a noise like a small trapped animal.
>
> 'What are you doing?' I asked.
>
> 'Ah, Billy, your mother is just checking my teeth', my father replied quickly, if not altogether convincingly.
>
> I believe you are supposed to be traumatised by these things. I can't remember being troubled at all, though it was some years before I let my mother look in my mouth again.

There's some sound advice available for Mums and Dads who have had their bedroom antics interrupted by the patter of tiny feet. In his book *How to Say the Right Thing Every Time*, Robert D. Ramsey recommends that parents should:

- Not over-react
- Set boundaries – 'next time knock first'
- Explain that grown-ups need special private time together

And about six months of counselling ought to do it.

Carnal language

It's not just the act of sex which causes us anxiety. The language of sex and associated body parts and other sexual paraphernalia is enough to send the blood pumping to our faces – and not from excitement.

I once set a young female BBC researcher the task of finding potential interviewees for a programme about new businesses springing up on the island of Shetland.

> 'There's a company making novelty pasta', she suggested. 'It comes in all sorts of shapes.'
> 'Such as?'
> Consulting the website, she read: 'Fish-shaped, star-shaped, ship-shaped ... er ... pennis-shaped.' She hesitated before adding: 'I'm not sure what that means.'
> 'Pennis-shaped?' I asked. 'Pennis? Like Dennis?'
> 'No – p.e.n.i.s', she corrected.
> 'That's penis-shaped then', I explained.

She blushed bright red, burning hot enough to toast marshmallows. I think I may have made things worse by tactlessly pointing this out.

Our sensitivity to the language of sex drives us to search for euphemisms to get us out of trouble. In preference to good old Anglo Saxon, we coyly plump for terms like 'bonking', 'sleeping together' or 'doing it' to describe the dirty deed (there we go again). I rather like Shakespeare's 'making the beast with two backs', though its application is not, unfortunately, apposite to the entire *Kama Sutra*.

In the 1970s, US comedian George Carlin launched a one-man campaign against linguistic censorship, sexual or otherwise, with his inspired rant about the 'seven words you will never hear on television'.

> There are some people that aren't into all the words. There are some people who would have you not use certain words. Yeah, there are 400,000 words in the English language, and there are seven of them that you can't say on television. What a ratio that is. 399,993 to

seven. They must really be bad. They'd have to be outrageous, to be separated from a group that large. All of you over here, you seven. Bad words. That's what they told us they were, remember? 'That's a bad word.' ... There are no bad words. Bad thoughts. Bad intentions.

And words, you know the seven don't you? Shit, Piss, Fuck, Cunt, Cocksucker, Motherfucker, and Tits, huh? Those are the heavy seven. Those are the ones that will infect your soul, curve your spine and keep the country from winning the war.

I have had more than a few battles down the years with BBC bosses who insisted I remove explicit sexual swear words from my radio features. I would protest, arguing: 'But that's what the Archbishop said', and 'Why do we have to sanitise everything?', but they would never budge. I would, inevitably, end up snipping the offending bit of tape from my programme.

In fact I still have a piece of paper pinned to my study wall which reads 'The Controller of Radio 4 can **** off.' The missing word is replaced by the one-inch-long piece of recording tape that the controller had required me to excise.

A final, slightly tangential thought about the language of sex. The great economist John Kenneth Galbraith learned at an early age that if you want to sexually proposition a young lady, you have to pick your words carefully, lest you be misunderstood.

How now?

'As a boy I lived on a farm in Canada', recalled J.K. Galbraith. 'On the adjoining farm lived a girl I was fond of. One day as we sat together on the top rail of the cattle pen we watched a bull servicing a cow. I turned to the girl, with what I hoped was a suggestive look, saying: 'That looks like it would be fun.' She replied: 'Well ... she's your cow.'

An erection in a nudist colony

Maybe we can learn something from naturists, who have, or at least claim to have, taken the sex out of nudity. By learning not to be embarrassed about our bodies, perhaps we can reduce our anxiety about sex in general.

The trouble with nudist colonies, at least for men, is the risk of having an erection. How embarrassing would that be? Well, naturists have considered the issue. Erections are rare, apparently, and the very fear of the embarrassment of getting an erection is normally enough to prevent the situation arising, so to speak.

And for those who, despite their best endeavours, still end up with an erection? Carry a towel, is the advice. Or a balloon?

And a naturist website offers this further advice.

> A male bathing nude in a swimming pool, hot tub, calm lake, or other still waters for the first time may be surprised to see his penis floating vertically in the water. Don't worry. Other nudists will not mistake this for an erection.

It's important to know these things. But there are other ways to embarrass oneself in a nudist colony, as one *Health and Efficiency* correspondent revealed.

> So I walked into the room and suddenly realised I had forgotten to take off my bra. Everyone laughed. I thought I'd just die from embarrassment.

And then there's the danger of an erection in a hospital.

A close shave

High school pupil Margot was sixteen when she enrolled in a New York student nursing programme. She spent an afternoon each week at the local hospital, assisting the nurses.

One day, she was asked to help shave a young male patient prior to his hernia operation. The potential for embarrassment was magnified by her discovery that the boy in question was someone she'd had a crush on at school for months.

The nurse began the delicate procedure, then handed Margot the razor and told her to finish the job. Nervously she began, but found that his penis kept getting in the way. 'Just pick it up with one hand and shave with the other', instructed the nurse. Margot thought she was going to faint, but did as she was told. And then it happened. The erection. Margot handed back the razor and began giving serious consideration to a career in accountancy.

For many men, of course, their problem is more to do with the failure to achieve an erection when one is actually required. I'll leave other, better qualified, people to advise on how that particular embarrassment can be avoided.

Illicit sex

While eating at an Indian restaurant with my family, I noticed a couple across the room having a romantic dinner. Holding hands across the table and staring into each other's eyes, they were totally blind to their biryanis.

The romantic spell was abruptly broken by the arrival of a wild-eyed woman who stormed into the restaurant, strode up to their table and proceeded to harangue the man, her husband, for his infidelity. She hated him, never wanted to see him again, the hussy was welcome to him, she'd chopped his best suits to ribbons ... etc., etc. She then turned on her heels and flounced out. Customers sat in shocked silence throughout the performance, embarrassment hanging in the air, thicker than the flock wallpaper. The 'couple' hung their heads, paid their bill and left. The room relaxed.

Australian novelist Kathy Lette once gained revenge on a two-timing boyfriend by stuffing his hollow curtain pole with prawns. Embarrassed by the mysterious smell of rotting fish, he eventually moved house – taking the pole with him.

Infidelity is, in almost every case, a sure-fire roadmap to embarrassment. Ask Baroness Thatcher's son Mark, whose wife Diane denounced him in the newspapers as a 'crooked cheat' after confronting him and one of his mistresses at a hotel. Or ask Chris Taylor ...

Up before the beak

Chris Taylor shared a flat in Leeds with his girlfriend Suzy Collins and his pet African grey parrot, Ziggy. What Chris didn't know, but Ziggy apparently did, was that, while he was out at work, Suzy was using the flat to entertain a young man called Gary. Suzy might have got away with the deception, if only Ziggy had learned to keep his big beak shut.

One evening Chris and Suzy were sitting together on the couch watching television and Ziggy blurted out: 'I love you Gary', perfectly mimicking Suzy's voice. Chris became suspicious. Who the hell was Gary? As if responding to Chris' unspoken question, Ziggy again cooed: 'I love you Gary', and added some slurpy kissing noises for effect.

Chris then remembered that Ziggy had recently called out 'Hiya Gary' when Suzy's mobile phone had rung. The penny dropped. Blushing red as beetroot, Suzy burst into tears and confessed her month-long affair. The next morning she packed her bags and left.

Shortly afterwards Chris had to part company with Ziggy too, having been driven to distraction by the bird's constant squawking of the name Gary in the voice of his ex-girlfriend.

Ziggy's exploits were widely reported by the BBC and most national newspapers. Other extraordinary tales of sexual embarrassment circulating on the internet can be dismissed as urban myths, or as jokes which have been taken literally. The following tale may fall into that category, though research reveals that it was reported some 30 years ago in *People*, so it *might* be true.

Caught in flagrante Ferrari

The early summer's evening air near London's Regent's Park was pierced by anguished cries for help. People rushing to the source of the commotion found a half-naked man and woman in the back of a small sports car. The man, it transpired, had slipped a disc in the middle of his athletic love-making. He was transfixed with pain.

Firemen arriving at the scene quickly established that the only way to get him out was to cut open the back of the car, which, in a blaze of oxyacetylene, they proceeded to do.

Before whisking the man off to hospital, ambulance-men reassured his girlfriend that he would make a full recovery. 'Never mind about him', the woman allegedly replied. 'I want to know how I'm supposed to explain to my husband what's happened to his car.'

While we're in the territory of the possibly apocryphal, there's this extraordinary incident, said to have occurred in an English criminal court.

I have a little note

The female complainant in a sexual assault case was asked to tell the court exactly how the defendant had propositioned her prior to the offence. Acutely embarrassed, she told the judge she simply couldn't say it out loud and asked if she could write it down instead. Granted permission, she scribbled a note which was then ceremoniously passed to the judge, and then on to the prosecuting counsel and then to the defence counsel and then to the jury. Each member of the jury read the note before handing it to his or her neighbour, until it arrived at a female juror who had briefly nodded off. She was nudged awake and handed the piece of paper. She read the note, looked at the man who had handed it to her, smiled coyly, refolded the note ... and placed it in her handbag.

The gender agenda

Our bodies are an endless source of embarrassment to us, whether or not we are trying to engage in sex. We'll look at this in more detail later, but for those who feel trapped in the body of a person of the wrong sex, very particular complications can emerge.

Oh sister

Writer and broadcaster Dylan Winter had just become the proud father of a bouncing baby girl. It was around the time that the comedy series *Blackadder* first hit our television screens, and that particular week's episode, set in Elizabethan times, revolved around the imperative of producing a male heir.

Inundated with calls asking after the health and sex of the new arrival, Dylan resorted to leaving the following message on his answerphone: 'To quote Nursey from *Blackadder*, "Thank the Lord it's a boy without a willy".'

The next person to phone the Winter household was Dylan's brother, who, following a sex-change operation, was now his sister.

'She was not', says Dylan, 'amused'.

Not in front of the cameras

We've already heard how filming sex and nudity scenes can lead to embarrassment. Indeed, it's difficult to imagine how it could be avoided, with or without the presence of a double-decker bus. Actress Julie Walters once famously insisted that an entire film crew, including the director, should strip naked, before she would take off her own clothes.

Ewan McGregor, when asked if he had ever become 'aroused' during the filming of a sex scene, confessed this had happened occasionally, but he just needed to be given a few minutes to compose himself before attempting another take.

Playing the role (I nearly wrote acting the part) of a spectacularly well-endowed porn star created a range of embarrassing situations for one American actor.

What's (more than) afoot?

In the film *Boogie Nights*, Mark Wahlberg played Dirk Diggler, a porn star whose penis measured nearly thirteen inches, as graphically revealed in the closing scene.

The prosthetic penis took half an hour to attach. 'I had a special effects technician (a penis-wrangler) to glue the thing on', he explained. 'I couldn't pee all day.'

Wahlberg says it was extremely embarrassing having his penis examined by people from make-up, wardrobe and special effects. After the film's release he had to tolerate men 'checking me out' in public urinals.

And what did Wahlberg's mother think of the film? 'I truly loved it', she declared. 'I think everything that was in the movie needed to be there.' [PAUSE] 'But I could have lived without the ending …'

A silver-framed photograph from that final scene does not, I'm fairly sure, sit on her living room mantelpiece alongside that of his high-school graduation.

* * *

Propensity to be embarrassed about sex is not evenly distributed by, er, gender, age or, indeed, national boundaries. I was astonished to discover that the Japanese, not satisfied with churning out appalling game shows involving ritual humiliation, have now come up with a television format which requires contestants to establish which of several women participants is a virgin. All done in the best possible taste, I'm sure.

While a fair way behind sexually liberated continental Europe, the British are working hard to shed their reputation for prudishness. Not only are there now more than 100 Ann Summers shops on the high streets, vibrators can be bought over the counter at Selfridges. Their best seller is a ceramic model called 'The Bone', which is, apparently, doing very good business at £199.

Perhaps we are slowly breaking down Freud's indivisible link between sex and anxiety. But will we ever see the Japanese *Spot the Virgin* programme, or its like, on British television screens? May the Lord Ofcom preserve us.

CHAPTER FOUR

LOVE, MARRIAGE
AND THE FAMILY WAY

Part One: A Froggie went a-courtin'

Our eyes meet across a crowded room, an assortment of
chemicals takes control of our brains – and we are undone.

The 'sex hormones' testosterone and oestrogen kick in first,
rapidly followed by chemicals which control attraction: dopa-
mine, adrenalin and most importantly, serotonin, considered
one of love's essential chemicals and one that might actually
send us temporarily insane. Temporary insanity would explain
why we have so much trouble with something which no less an
authority than the Jackson Five insist is as easy as ABC.

Let's be honest, I was no teenage Romeo. Girls didn't call to
me from their balconies, or if they did it was only to tell me
where to leave the groceries.

At around the age of fifteen I started going to nightclubs in
the West End of London, where disco-scarred young madams
would respond to invitations to dance by saying: 'Sorry, I've
got a wooden leg.' I was naive enough to believe them the first
few times, until it dawned on me that either the club was
having a special 'half-price for one-legged women' night, or,
fractionally more likely, I was being given the brush-off.

I am not, of course, the only froggie to have struggled with his a-courtin'.

Pond life

Michael Magenis was eighteen years old and unrequitedly attracted to a young lady whom we shall call Ophelia, for reasons which will become apparent.

Arriving at a party one Saturday evening, he couldn't believe his luck when he was warmly greeted by the fair object of his affections. After drinking more than was good for either of them, they decided to go for a stroll in the dimly lit back garden.

In a moment of alcohol-fuelled enthusiasm, Michael offered to carry his date over the muddy grass to a drier patch beyond. Sweeping her off her feet before she could protest, he took several precarious steps before it dawned on him that he was wading into a small pond. Surprised by the sudden cold and dampness, he took complete leave of his senses, and, alas, his grip on young Ophelia, and firmly deposited her in the pond.

Recovering a little, he gallantly dragged her out of the water, depositing her on the grass, soaking wet, covered in pond weed and frogspawn.

Despite this astonishingly embarrassing start to their relationship, five years later Michael and his mucky mermaid got married, and today laugh merrily when they tell their grandchildren the 'pond story'.

Wouldn't it be wonderful if that last bit were true?

In reality the 'pond story' resulted in the instant termination of Michael and Ophelia's relationship, leaving him with nothing but a damp and painful memory. From a distance all the danger signals were there, but Michael was just too close to events, and, clearly, too drunk, to spot them. Embarrassment-evasion requires a clear and sober head, and the strict avoidance of dimly lit gardens, fish ponds and heavy lifting. Still we can all learn from Michael's misfortune, as well as from that of other lovelorn losers.

Except we won't, of course. Love, after all, is blind – not least to the potential for embarrassment.

In the land of Mills and Boon, the path of true love follows a predictable pattern – boy meets girl, boy loses girl, boy regains girl. In the real world the pattern is more often, boy meets girl, boy and girl have an embarrassing time and never see each other again.

Padding about

Erin was being taken out to dinner in a rather nice restaurant by her rather nice new boyfriend. Beneath her silk blouse she was wearing a slightly padded push-up bra. She wanted to look her perkiest.

Starters came and went without incident. But while they were waiting for the main course, an almond-shaped piece of black padding somehow worked its way out of her bra and slithered onto the empty white plate in front of her.

Her boyfriend looked, then looked away. He said nothing. Mortified, Erin clawed the offending object into her handbag and rushed, lopsidedly, to the toilets to replace it.

It was, sadly, their last date.

It's a strange but interesting fact that most teenage girls (and I've done my research here) will go to great lengths to avoid eating in front of their boyfriends. For reasons which are not altogether clear to me, they find the prospect embarrassing, and not just because of the risk of getting gravy on their chins or spinach in their teeth. Eating just isn't cool.

Lydia, unfortunately, had grown out of that stage.

Choking not joking

Jeff was perfect. He owned an art gallery, was intelligent, distinguished and now, finally, had asked Lydia out to dinner.

The food at the posh French restaurant was delicious. The wine and the conversation flowed. On top of everything else, Jeff was funny. Over dessert he suddenly said: 'Enough about me; I want to hear from you. What do *you* think about *me*?' Lydia, who had just taken a bite of cake, burst out laughing, and then began to choke.

Gulping down water didn't help. Jeff, leaping to the rescue, attempted the Heimlich manoeuvre, but that didn't work either. A woman at the next table told Jeff he was doing it all wrong, and took over. Lydia was nearly passing out, but remembers thinking that she had finally got a decent date and was going to choke to death. How could things possibly get worse?

The woman gave Lydia another firm jerk under the ribcage and finally dislodged the lump of food, which, along with the rest of the contents of her stomach, came gushing out … all over Jeff.

I have an endless supply of embarrassing stories involving vomit, but I'll spare you them. There was definitely no throwing up on this next date, indeed very little activity of any kind.

Knock-out date

US actress Beth Broderick may have qualified for the Guinness Book of Records for going on the briefest date ever. Invited out by a man she had met in the gym, they arrived at a restaurant and sat down at their table. He looked into her eyes and said: 'I've been watching you for a year and I never thought you'd go out with me.' He then promptly fainted. Beth was, she says, dumbfounded.

And yet here's a date that almost ended before it started.

Drive-into restaurant

TV presenter Denise Van Outen had been invited out for a meal by a chap she really fancied. She'd just passed her driving test and offered to pick him up so she could show off her new set of wheels. As they entered the restaurant car park, Denise was concentrating more on flirting than driving, hit the accelerator instead of the brake and ploughed straight into the side of the building. The car was a write-off, but the restaurant and, miraculously, the date, survived.

* * *

Sorry may be the hardest word. But 'will you go out with me?' is the hardest question. Many relationships never have the chance to blossom into embarrassing disaster, because fear of rejection robs young lovers of the power of speech. American comedian Dom Irrera knows the pain of the putdown. 'I asked this one girl out', he recalls, 'and she said, "You got a friend?" I said yes. She said, "Then go out with him."'

No rhapsody

While visiting Havana one year, the American composer George Gershwin was stood up by a young woman for a lunch date. Later that afternoon he spotted her on the yacht club terrace. 'Hey!' he exclaimed, 'you stood me up!' 'Oh, I meant to phone and tell you I couldn't meet you', the woman replied apologetically. 'But do you know something? I couldn't remember your name!'

Gershwin didn't recover for days.

Psychotherapist Albert Ellis was a shy nineteen-year-old, and ashamed of his shyness, which made things worse. Resolving to break free from this spiral of shame, he forced himself to spend a day in New York's Botanical Gardens, attempting to engage in conversation every eligible-looking woman who walked by. By the end of the day, Ellis had conquered his social handicap and begun his new life as a Don Juan.

It's that simple.

For those who don't fancy the botanical gardens option, there's always computer dating. The initial risk of humiliating rejection is effectively removed, but the potential for other forms of embarrassment is mortifyingly multiplied. This anonymous internet blogger posted a brief résumé of just a few of her catastrophic computer dates.

My list of losers

1. The man who claimed his sense of humour was his greatest asset and demonstrated it by doing Groucho Marx imitations all through dinner at a fancy restaurant.
2. The man who said he saw a 'daddy' when he looked in the mirror and asked (on the first and only date) if I was ovulating.

3. The man who demanded a list of the 'specific skills and strengths' that I could bring to a relationship, as well as an analysis of the 'self-destructive patterns' that caused my divorce.
4. The man whose first words were 'I'm sorry, I've got to concentrate on getting well tonight', and who spent most of the evening stuffing Vicks Vaporub up his nose.

And those, she says, were among her more successful dates.

Forty-four-year-old Liz Franklin admits she brought online dating embarrassment upon herself.

Nailing her man

Liz Franklin turned to computer dating in an attempt to get back 'out there' after the collapse of her twenty-year marriage. After a series of disastrous dates, she arranged to meet John from Essex. He seemed funny and interesting on the phone, but she wasn't too thrilled when he suggested a Sainsbury's cafe for the rendezvous. 'But it occurred to me that if he didn't turn up, or was hideous, at least I could do a bit of shopping', she says. He did turn up and was, apparently, '6ft 4in of drop-dead dishyness'. Liz takes up the story:

> Across the table he held my hand again and we chatted and laughed, sharing our food without any awkwardness. I reached over and walked my fingers playfully up his shirtsleeves a little way and rested them there until it was time to go. I felt sure it was the start of something quite special. As I withdrew my hands, two of my stick-on nails

chose to part company with my fingers and attach themselves to the hair on his forearms. Whether or not this ruined the connection, I'll never know. But he didn't ask to see me again.

And she hasn't worn false nails since.

American comedienne Rita Mae Brown was once asked what she thought of computer dating. 'It's terrific', she replied, 'if you're a computer.'

Meet the parents

Around the age of sixteen, still struggling for success with the opposite sex, I developed the tactic of pretending I was older than I was – claiming to be studying A-levels rather than O-levels, for example. And on one remarkable occasion it actually worked. The young lady concerned was really the same age as me, but she believed I was a sophisticated two years her senior. Our conversation rarely strayed onto academic matters, so it was easy to maintain the pretence – until she invited me home to meet the parents. Mum and Dad were, alas, unhealthily interested in my school life and quizzed me closely about the subjects I was studying and the books I was reading for English Literature. I did my best, but they knew I was lying, and I knew they knew, and they knew that I knew that they knew. It wasn't a very comfortable experience. It came as no great surprise when, later, their daughter failed to return my calls.

There are various internet versions of the almost certainly apocryphal story of Debbie, who, while on a visit to meet her boyfriend's parents, went in search of the lavatory. She found a bathroom but it didn't seem to have a toilet, just a wash basin. In desperation she tried to climb onto it, but it broke from its moorings, sending her crashing against a wall. Her prospective in-laws found her semi-conscious on the floor in a pool of water. Several months later, so the story goes, she was again invited to her boyfriend's parents' home. On this occasion all went well until she got up from the table, stepped on the family's beloved shih-tzu and broke the dog's neck. True or not, it's easy to see from where the film *Meet the Parents* got its inspiration.

These following accounts of meeting the parents come from impeccable sources.

Hold your horses

Lisa Smith was dating her first serious boyfriend. On one occasion he suggested they pop round to his parents' home to pick up his wallet en route to the cinema.

They went in and Lisa was introduced to his mother, who got straight to the point, saying: 'Hello love, nice to meet you, I know you'll make my lad very happy.' Lisa was somewhat 'freaked out', considering she was only sixteen and had been dating the woman's son for only three weeks.

At subsequent meetings, her boyfriend's mother would waste no opportunity to bring up the subjects of engagement parties, wedding dresses or babies. 'How cute are these little booties? They come in blue and pink', she would say.

One Saturday Lisa was invited round to dinner to meet Granny and Grandpa. The conversation took a deeply disturbing turn: 'We do hope you are using protection. Rings on fingers before babies', she was instructed.

Lisa ended the relationship the next day.

Stand-up comic Josie Long was only seventeen when she won the BBC New Comedy Award. A year or two later she took her boyfriend Matthew to meet her mother. It was an excruciatingly embarrassing event which she subsequently recorded in a poem, first published in an anthology of comedians' poetry, called *That Which Is Not Said*.

The First Time My Mum Met My Boyfriend

We went to a Turkish restaurant
And I didn't have enough money to pay so she treated us.
I wanted her to be stiff and semi-formal
and for the whole thing to be like it was in the 1950s.
I started conversations about how he was a teacher
but she had to bring up the men she was meeting
from an advert she put in the 'news shopper'
and I ate tsatsiki and looked down at the table
while she said
'I mean, one didn't have any testicles
and the other had false teeth!
What am I supposed to do?
Choose between testicles and teeth?
What would you choose Matthew?'
and I spat out a bit of kofte.
He tried to respond
but it wasn't what my mum wanted to hear.
And she said to me
'What do you think I should do dear?'
and I didn't know where I could start.
So I said
'The food is really good isn't it,
Have you had one of these aubergines?'

The following X-rated story, posted on the internet by a Nevada dental receptionist, is almost too terrible to be true.

Meet mother

Patty was going out on a blind date with Peter, a friend of a friend. He took her to a nice restaurant and all was fine until the conversation turned to the subject of his mother. 'You look quite a lot like my mother ... you laugh the way my mother laughs ... my mother would love you ... you must meet Mother.' It was more than a little disconcerting.

Driving her home, he suddenly announced that he was going to take her to see his mother. Ignoring her protests that it was far too late, he drove for miles towards the outskirts of town, before finally pulling up in an unlit driveway.

They got out and stumbled a little in the dark before Peter suddenly stopped and said: 'Oh, there you are, Mother ... Mother, meet Patty ... Patty, meet my mother.'

He was talking to a tombstone.

Norman Bates lives.

Breaking up is hard to do

Some first dates are less disastrous, of course, and can even lead to lasting relationships. But embarrassment is never far away, and crashes in again when those relationships go pear-shaped, or simply run out of steam.

Telephone termination

Actor Adam Sandler has made a career out of playing social misfits. Perhaps it has something to do with his childhood.

He tells the story of how, when he was in the sixth grade, the telephone rang while his family was having dinner. It was Kim from school. 'See that?' said Sandler to his Dad. 'The girls are calling.'

But it turned out that Kim was phoning to tell him that the girl he was dating wanted to break up with him. Kim was sorry to be the bearer of bad news.

Sandler recalls: 'I walked back to the table, and my Dad says, "How'd that go?" I said, "Good." He said, "What'd she say?" I told him, "She said she was looking forward to seeing me tomorrow." He said, "All right. Good job." And then I stared at my plate and tried not to cry the whole dinner.'

Adam Sandler took his rejection like a man. Mandy Jones' boyfriend took it like a spoiled child.

Temper tantrum

A few months after Mandy Jones agreed to let Jeffrey Evans move in to her home in Gwent in South Wales, she realised she had made a big mistake. She couldn't cope with his over-possessive behaviour and told him to pack his bags.

Three weeks later, Mandy discovered that Evans had taken his revenge. He'd produced a poster headlined 'Randy Mandy', displaying a topless photograph he had taken of her during a recent holiday in Turkey, and a list of explicit sexual favours (and prices) followed by her home phone number. He had plastered it on every lamp-post, tree and shop window and in every telephone box and public toilet in Mandy's neighbourhood.

Mandy raced around the streets tearing down posters wherever she could find them. When she got home there was already a message waiting on her answerphone. 'Is this Randy Mandy?' a gruff voice said. 'I'm interested in your personal services.' It was the first of many calls.

Jeffrey Evans didn't get away with humiliating his former lover. He was eventually arrested, charged with five counts of harassment and the theft of Mandy Jones' mobile phone, and jailed for eight months.

American actress Diane Farr came up with a cunning, but far less extreme, plan to turn the tables and embarrass her fiancé when he broke off their engagement.

Enragement cards

When actress Diane Farr got engaged in 2002, she sent out 300 announcement cards to inform her friends and relatives. It had the word 'ENGAGED' in big bold letters and their names underneath it.

When, six weeks later, her fiancé called off the engagement, Diane was upset and embarrassed. She came up with a form of revenge aimed at throwing the embarrassment back on him. She printed another 300 cards, this time with the word 'SINGLE' and the message: 'Picked the wrong guy, gave him the wrong finger! Thanks for your support.'

Diane got so much positive feedback that she ended up starting a greeting card company. Forty-two-year-old Fran from Phoenix, Arizona, had no warning that the end was nigh.

Getting the chop

Fran and her boyfriend had been dating for about six months and everything seemed to be going very well. One day he arrived at her home and announced that he would prepare dinner, and then went out to buy some lamb chops.

Half an hour later, the phone went. 'I'm at the butcher's shop', said her boyfriend. 'I'll make it quick. I've fallen in love with a woman I've met in the queue. I'm not coming back.'

On top of that, she had to make her own dinner. Temporary insanity indeed.

Perhaps some of these people should have subscribed to the services of a new German 'separation agency'. For a modest fee, a 52-year-old former insurance salesman called Bernd Dressler will inform your partner that the relationship is over. Herr Dressler, nicknamed The Terminator, offers a range of services from 'sensitive phone call' at 13 euros to a 'personalised home visit' at upwards of 50 euros, which includes a detailed explanation as to why his client has decided to end the relationship. The follow-up service includes discreet collection of the client's belongings from a former lover's home. If only there were agencies to bail us out of all the embarrassing situations we generate for ourselves.

Some relationships don't collapse outright; they just teeter on the edge.

Food for thought

Film producer and screenwriter Nunnally Johnson once arrived at a restaurant to have lunch with his girlfriend, quite unaware that she intended to air various grievances about their relationship.

Johnson ordered his favourite dish (herring roe) into which he was heartily tucking when the emotional scene began to unfold. Unwilling to abandon his beloved roe, he attempted, between mouthfuls, to make appropriate sounds of contrition and apology.

'Look at you!' his girlfriend finally cried, furious at his inattention. 'Our very lives are at the crossroads! And you sit there smacking your lips like a pig!'

'I'm so sorry', Johnson replied. 'If I'd known it was going to be like this, I'd have ordered something I didn't like!'

Relationships which survive such crises will often (though statistically less often than in the past) stumble towards a proposal of marriage. Here the man (it still usually is the man) again risks the embarrassment of rejection. One solution is to make the proposal so public that the object of your affections has no choice but to say yes.

In May 2005 country music star Garth Brooks proposed to his 'best friend' of twenty years, Trisha Yearwood, on stage in front of 7,000 cheering fans. She said yes. Others pop the question via giant billboards, or sky-writing, or courtesy of the pilot of a transatlantic airliner. 'This is your captain speaking. We are flying at an altitude of 35,000 feet and will arrive in Miami in approximately 90 minutes. And by the way, a message for Judith in row 49. Peter would like to know if you would do him the honour of marrying him.' How could a girl refuse? Between periods at an American basketball game, a man took the microphone and proposed to his girlfriend. The girl's reply could not be heard, but the scoreboard flashed: 'She said NO.' The crowd gasped as the woman ran off the court. It turned out that it was just a stunt, involving actors, staged to promote a 'fan proposal' service at $200 a pop. But it could happen.

Actually it did once happen, to a woman who proposed to her partner on Dutch TV, only to be humiliatingly turned down. Gerda Goermaat had told her boyfriend Henk De Voorst of her intention to appear on *Welcome to Your Wedding*, and he had warned her that he would refuse to marry her on live television. She thought he was bluffing.

According to wedding planners, women almost always say yes, rather than embarrass their suitor. It's only later, in private, that they back out.

Actress Brenda Blethyn once, sort of, proposed on the phone.

Crank proposal

Award-winning British actress Brenda Blethyn has been living happily with her partner, Michael Mayhew, for more than 30 years. Neither has ever really felt the need to get married.

Except perhaps once, a few years ago, when Brenda was working in America and was missing Michael. She'd had a drink or two, and forgetting it was three o'clock in the morning back in Britain, picked up the phone and called home.

A sleepy voice answered the phone. 'Michael', said Brenda. 'I've been thinking. Why don't you and me get married.'

There was a pause before Michael replied: 'Who is this?'

Part Two: For God's sake get me to the church

I married beneath me. All women do.
                            Nancy Astor

With luck you will circumvent all the potential pitfalls and disasters of romance, strike lucky, and fix the wedding date. No respite here, I'm afraid. They don't call them 'blushing brides' for nothing.

First you have to negotiate the hen or stag night, with associated strippers, spiked drinks and waking up naked, handcuffed to a lamp post; or worse, waking up naked, handcuffed to a stripper.

Such events are always embarrassing, and sometimes go way beyond that.

Light pink touchpaper

Ambulanceman Mark Myers was on duty one night in May 2006, when reports came in of a person set on fire in the toilet of a pub in Hackney.

Arriving at the scene, he discovered that the man was the victim of a stag-night prank. 'His so-called friends had thought it hilarious to dress him as a mummy, wrapping him from head to foot in toilet paper', says Mark. 'One of them then decided it would be even funnier to set fire to the toilet paper, badly underestimating its flammability.' Unable to put out the flames, his friends then rushed him into the toilet in search of water. By the time Mike's ambulance and other emergency services arrived at the scene, the flames were out, but the groom had suffered serious burns. The wedding was postponed.

For those who arrive uncharred at the altar, there are still plenty of ways for what should be the happiest day of one's life to turn into the most embarrassing.

Guardian columnist Michael Horden admits to a history of causing embarrassing scenes at weddings, including 'spilling red wine over a woman with a white dress' and starting a fight with her husband.

Once he attended a friend's wedding where someone else, for a change, was causing the embarrassment. The father of the bride was making his speech. 'Today you are married', he began. 'I just hope to God it works out.' What followed was a 25-minute attack on love and marriage. Explained Michael: 'The man in question had recently divorced from the bride's mother and was not about to let his daughter's happiness stand in the way of his own emotional bile. It was an astonishing thing to behold.'

And immensely embarrassing. But this is probably trumped by a speech at a wedding in Luton, at which the best man went dramatically over the top, stunning his audience with tales of the groom's sexual prowess and how he had scored with the stripper at his stag night. The bride ran screaming from the room and didn't speak to her husband for several months.

Wedding receptions are natural theatres of embarrassment. One friend confesses that after drinking nine pints at one reception, he asked one of the bridesmaids to dance and managed to break her foot. Another said he had recently attended a wedding but left early after someone started punching the DJ.

Ian Gittins is the author of *Weddings from Hell*, a collection of all-too-true stories from around the world, many of which featured in the Granada television series of the same name. 'There was one case in England', says Gittins, 'where the groom had given his video camera to a friend to film the ceremony so they could all watch it at the party that night. The groom had forgotten that he had used the tape in question to film himself having sex with his neighbour's dog, footage of which was then shown to the guests. He ended up being convicted of gross indecency.'

A couple getting married in Wales ran into problems before the ceremony had even begun.

Wedding ring ring

When the organist failed to turn up at the wedding of Terry Moore and Sharon Pearson in Merthyr Tydfil, a friend of the groom came to the rescue. His mobile phone, by a happy coincidence, included the wedding march as one of its ring tone options. His number had to be dialled several times before the happy couple made it to the altar.

Well, it was better than the Crazy Frog. Meanwhile in America...

Getting the bird

A Californian couple planned a romantic outdoor wedding at which they would exchange vows underneath a purpose-built gazebo. Scores of doves would then be released from inside its roof. Unfortunately most of the birds succumbed to the mid-summer sun and fell, stone-dead, on the heads of the happy couple.

And wedding blues – Turkish style...

No Turkish delight

A guest at a Turkish wedding reception turned up late, drunk and determined to enact the traditional local custom of firing live bullets into the air to celebrate the marriage. Unfortunately he ended up shooting the bride in the foot and a man in the stomach. The guest was promptly arrested and the nineteen-year-old bride spent her wedding night in hospital.

My cousin Stephen didn't know quite what he had let himself in for when he agreed to get married abroad.

Games people play

Stephen Winston fell in love with Ellen, an investment trader from Hong Kong, and romantically proposed on a ski slope in Switzerland.

The wedding and reception, in Hong Kong, was a model of oriental elegance – that is until Ellen's friend Kennix announced it was time to play *the wedding games*.

The first required Ellen to sit holding a piece of paper, while Stephen painted the Chinese character for 'love' with a long marker ... held between his thighs. The wedding video dwells on the faces of Stephen's family and friends looking suitably embarrassed. But they've seen nothing yet.

Kennix then produced a pastry, a 'Chinese Puff', filled with cream, which he placed delicately on Ellen's lap. Stephen was then instructed to kneel in front of her and lick the cream from the pastry.

The video again reveals the reaction of the English guests. This time they all have their eyes fixed firmly on their own food, intent, it seems, on mastering the technique of using chopsticks.

Stephen claims not to have been unduly embarrassed, distracted somewhat by the fact that the cream in the Chinese Puff tasted of Thousand Island dressing.

* * *

And for those considering breaking their wedding vows, a couple of salutary tales. Mary-Jo Eustace, a Canadian television presenter whose husband left her after twelve years for the actress Tori Spelling, promptly wrote a book called *My Husband Left Me for Tori Spelling*. And Pavla Topolánek, the wife of the Czech Prime Minister, Mirek, decided to run for an opposition party after her husband had an affair with the deputy head of parliament.

You have been warned.

Part Three: The family way

It happened in a small theatre on the fringe of the Edinburgh Fringe. An aspiring stand-up comedian was dying on his feet. Hostile elements in the audience were yelling at him to get off. In abject misery, the hapless comic peered out into the gloom to try to identify a particularly persistent heckler sitting near the front. It was his mother. She was shouting: 'Don't slouch!'

It seems to me that our families ought to offer us some protection from embarrassment; they should provide an environment in which we can say and do what we want, within reason, without being judged and condemned. In reality the family, with its uncool parents, precocious and competing children, dotty grandparents and loopy aunts and uncles, tends to create a hotbed of humiliation for, um, all the family.

Many parents, convinced that their newborn children are destined to become a source of embarrassment to them, seem determined to get their retaliation in first, punishing their innocent offspring in advance by giving them unbelievably stupid names.

What else would explain the decision of Mr and Mrs Pipe to call their bouncing baby boy 'Dwayne', or Bill Lear (founder of the Lear Jet Corporation) and his wife Moya to call their daughter 'Shanda'?

I confess my wife and I had seriously considered calling our firstborn son Joe, until the consequences occurred to us. And my parents had been married for more than 25 years before my father admitted to my mother, at a family party, that he had not, as she had been led to believe, been christened George Edwin King, but Fritz Kreisler King, after the popular violinist of the time.

But it's celebrity parents who seem most keen to inflict embarrassing names on their children. Frank Zappa set something of a trend by naming his daughter Moon Unit. But Bob Geldof and Paula Yates qualify as multiple offenders, conferring the names Fifi Trixibelle, Peaches Honeyblossom and Little Pixie on their daughters. Paula Yates later named her daughter with Michael Hutchence, Heavenly Hiraani Tiger Lily.

It's hard to say how much, if any, emotional damage this causes. Perhaps the children all grow up tougher and more resilient, as in 'A Boy Named Sue'. Then again, maybe not. If, as we have discussed, our innate instinct is to hide within the herd, then having to roam the social savannahs with the name Heavenly Hiraani is not going to help.

A few years back, the fashion for giving offspring unusual names became so popular in Peru that a law (subsequently revoked) was enacted banning the practice. It had been argued that children were being psychologically damaged by such names as McDonalds Huaman, Michael Jackson Quispe and Patricia Neurona H20 Poggi.

This casual cruelty has been going on for a long time. Researchers looking into Cornish public records have come up with the Gurney family of Endellion who, back in 1741, named their child 'Offspring'; and the Guy family from Helston who in 1800 opted to call their son 'Guy'. This may have been what inspired the grandparents of England footballers Gary and Philip Neville to name their son Neville.

While the incidence of silly first names seems to be on the increase, the good news is that embarrassing surnames are on the decline. A study of 20,000 surnames over five generations has revealed that Cocks, Willys, Dafts, Smellies and Shufflebottoms are fading away, ditched by their owners through marriage or deed poll. Also, you'll be pleased to learn, there are far fewer Nutters around.

* * *

A major survey of 1,000 primary-school children placed 'being kissed at the school gates' as among the most embarrassing things parents can do, though 'being told off in public' came a close second. Being named Jason or Kylie didn't figure.

The authors of the survey, commissioned for some reason by the manufacturers of Jammie Dodger biscuits, say it shows that adults who shudder at the memory of their parents' behaviour are now doing the same thing to their own offspring.

The clothes worn by parents of both sexes were highlighted as another major source of embarrassment, as was their choice of family car. The great majority of the children felt they could have made better choices themselves.

Parents in the North East were voted the most embarrassing in Britain, and Welsh parents the least. One in five Welsh children actually described their parents as 'cool'. Until they start singing, presumably.

John Peel, in his sadly unfinished memoirs, recalls being

frequently embarrassed by his over-demonstrative mother. On one particular occasion, when he was seven years old, she took him to the outfitters' department of Browns of Chester, determined to draw attention to what she considered to be his *deformity*.

Avast behind

Arriving in the Boys' Uniform sector of Browns she sought assurances, in a booming voice, from the staff members who scurried obsequiously forward to offer assistance, that clothing could be found that would adequately cover what she characterised as an excessively large backside. As she shouted these, her thoughts, the centre of Chester came to a standstill. Like something from an H.M. Bateman cartoon, I would shrivel almost to nothingness as other customers and members of staff craned to see the malformed body part and its unfortunate owner, doors to Accounts Departments and Managers' Offices would open and people would peer out, careworn faces eager with anticipation of what was likely to prove the day's only laugh.

Your parents bring you up to be respectful towards them, but sometimes they make it very difficult.

Pyjama game

Nick Fer and some friends were playing strip poker. His parents, he believed, were safely tucked up in bed, fast asleep. In the small hours his angry father burst into the room, catching the group in various stages of undress. He launched into a long lecture about 'appropriate behaviour', the force of which was somewhat undermined by the fact that his pyjama flies were gaping open and his penis was hanging out.

Yorkshire poet Simon Armitage could be forgiven for concealing the circumstances of his mortification, but instead, he chose to share them.

Poetic injustice

Simon Armitage was disappointed to see a volume of his poetry selling for 10p in a bin outside a charity shop. Picking up the book, he noticed it was a signed copy. But there was worse to come. Beside the signature, in his own handwriting, was the inscription: 'To Mum and Dad.'

Getting their own back

Children, bless them – don't you just love the cute things they say and do? Except when they embarrass you, of course.

Writer and broadcaster Jenni Mills was about three or four years old when she wandered away from her parents during a trip to Birmingham's Botanical Gardens and found her way onto the bandstand. Passers-by, spotting her standing there, started to applaud.

'So I sang the only song I knew, called "I Hear Thunder"', she recalls. 'There was more applause, so I did a little dance, curtseyed, and sang it again. More applause. I was going to go for a second encore, but spotted that my father was glowering at me – and decided it might be a good idea to call it a day.'

Her father, a very private man, was embarrassed by his daughter's exhibitionism. 'I had drawn attention to myself and by extension to him', explains Jenni.

My son Dan, aged about six, on a coach trip from Jerusalem to Masada in Israel, was briefly adopted by a young girl, an American student who played with him during the long journey. All was fine until Dan, without warning, plunged his head down the front of her fluffy mohair jumper. Her embarrassment was total. Mine, I confess, was tinged with jealousy. Dan's, of course, was non-existent.

Have mercy

Actress Diana Dors, like most mothers, had to deal with her young sons coming home trying out swear words they had learned in the playground. And like any good mother, she went to great lengths to teach them that nice people didn't use such words.

One Sunday she took her boys to church and the vicar, delivering his sermon, was explaining that, even in our deepest and darkest adversity, God would be there, caring for our souls.

The congregation's respectful silence was pierced by one of Diana's darlings who stood up, pointed an accusing finger at the vicar, and shouted: 'You see Mummy. *He* said arseholes.'

Woman's Hour presenter Jenni Murray was on a P&O ferry travelling from the south coast to France with her four-year-old son Ed and baby Charlie. They were sitting in the restaurant when Ed piped up, in a voice which would have competed with the ship's foghorn: 'Mum, you know when you and Dad made Charlie – did he put his willy in your mouth or your bottom?'

Jenni blames herself for being too honest with her children on the subject of sex education. Sticking to storks and gooseberry bushes is generally much safer.

Sometimes the family embarrassment business can turn into a game of tit-for-tat, as in the case of this widely reported story.

Anything you can do

Steve Williams became so fed up with his daughter's messy bedroom that he built a website featuring pictures of her accumulating detritus, in the hope of embarrassing her into action. Within a fortnight his daughter Claire's version of Tracey Emin's *Unmade Bed* had been viewed by 40,000 people around the world.

Twenty-year-old business student Claire (obviously still a teenager at heart), was not amused, but it did spur her into doing a bit of tidying-up – while she planned her revenge. With the help of her father's friends, she set up a rival website displaying photos of him in a variety of compromising situations. One showed him drunk and dancing around with a handbag at a party. Another, of his garage, revealed his own untidiness – and his hypocrisy.

A case of MAE – Mutually Assured Embarrassment.

* * *

When it suits them, politicians don't hesitate to use their families to gain some sort of advantage. Kissing, and indeed having, babies is always a vote-winner. A pretty wife and smiling children look good on the hustings and it's certainly beneficial to have your family clustering around you while you deny accusations of an extramarital affair.

But there's a downside to political parenthood.

Tony Blair was probably not delighted when his son Euan was arrested for being drunk and incapable in London's Leicester Square after celebrating the end of his GCSE exams. Similarly, Jack Straw, when Home Secretary, could have done without his seventeen-year-old son attempting to sell cannabis to a newspaper reporter. And it's unlikely that George W. Bush, with his own history of alcohol problems, welcomed the revelations that his daughters had been caught indulging in a spot of under-age drinking.

In the summer of 2006, the offspring of quite a few US politicians took part in an internet-based version of throwing their toys out of the pram. In what seemed to be a coordinated temper tantrum, they began posting highly compromising messages and photographs on MySpace internet sites.

Among those embarrassed was Republican Congressman Louie Gohmert. His standing as a politician and district judge was scarcely enhanced by the discovery of internet pictures of his daughter Caroline dancing on a bar top and posing with a man in his underpants. The leader of the Republican Party in the US Senate, Senator Bill Frist, has always maintained a restrained position on Iraq. So pictures of his son Jonathan, dressed up as a suicide bomber, wearing six cans of beer strapped to his belt, were not helpful. Nor was the online profile posted by his other son Bryan, who wrote: 'I was born an American by God's amazing grace. Let's bomb some people.'

In the embarrassment war-zone that is the family, no prisoners are taken and few combatants emerge unscathed.

CHAPTER FIVE

SOCIAL DISGRACES

We are, the vast majority of us anyway, social creatures. We instinctively seek the company of others, craving their admiration and support. Without it we tend to fall apart, becoming insecure and depressed. Pathetic really.

It's this dependence on fellow human beings that makes us so vulnerable to embarrassment. If we behaved like other, more solitary animals, we could avoid a lot of grief. We should be more like the snake, orang-utan or lobster, which prefer to slither, swing or swim in splendid isolation. Lobsters (who really do swim, albeit backwards) shun the company of other crustaceans, almost never display signs of embarrassment, and go red only when plunged into boiling water.

If we steer clear of other people, we can escape embarrassment. Embarrassment needs an audience. Unlike shame, which can be experienced in total isolation, embarrassment requires us to be observed, or at least to feel as if we have been observed. The philosophers ask: 'If a tree falls in a forest and no one hears it, does it make a sound? To which I say: 'I haven't a clue.' But if they were to ask: 'If a man slips on a banana skin in the forest and no one sees him, is it embarrassing?', I can reply, unequivocally: 'No.'

83

I could easily have avoided any embarrassment about my most recent act of gross stupidity – making a 30-minute, three-train tube journey to get from London's Covent Garden to Aldwych, a distance of only 300 yards on foot – had I not admitted it here.

One route to a life less mortified is to become a hermit, having contact with other people only when absolutely essential and never ever going to Hollywood film awards.

That scent you're wearing …

In 1996 British actress Brenda Blethyn was nominated for a Golden Globe for her role in the Mike Leigh film *Secrets and Lies*. She turned up at the Beverly Hills ceremony wearing a glamorous designer frock adorned with a large, ornate brooch. Waiting for the Best Actress category, her nerves got the better of her, necessitating a dash to the washroom. Struggling to get out of her tight-fitting dress, she managed to break the brooch and, leaning forward to pick up the pieces, succeeded in peeing over her dress.

Damp, slightly dishevelled and close to tears, she made her way back to her table. The Best Actress category came round, but she was absolutely convinced she would not win. She was wrong. The spotlight followed her as she made her way nervously towards the stage and the open arms of one of Hollywood's leading actors, who was waiting to present her award. But there was just one thing on Brenda's mind … how well developed was Nicolas Cage's sense of smell?

Most of us don't need to be soaked in our own urine to suffer embarrassment. Just trying a little bit too hard to elevate ourselves up the social pecking order will do it.

One is not having it

As wife of the *Sunday Times* proprietor, Lady Kemsley was desperate to be on social terms with King George V and Queen Mary. In response to repeated grovelling requests, Queen Mary finally agreed to visit the Kemsley mansion for tea. It was made very clear to Lady Kemsley that on such a private visit, coverage by the *Sunday Times* or any other of her husband's newspapers would be quite inappropriate.

But Lady Kemsley did not want her social elevation to go unrecorded, so she discreetly concealed a *Sunday Times* photographer in one of the trees which lined her main drive. His task was to take a discreet picture of Queen Mary being greeted at the front door by her hostess.

But the photographer was not a young man. The day was warm and, during his vigil in the tree, he nodded off to sleep. As Queen Mary's limousine entered the front gate, the unfortunate man and his camera fell directly into its path.

Lady Kemsley, at her front door, watched the Royal vehicle carefully avoid the fallen photographer, turn in a wide arc and go back out of the front gate again, never to return.

For a species so reliant on intimacy, we are extraordinarily bad at interacting with each other, possessed of an infinite capacity to say and do the wrong things.

Embarrassment is the British default emotion. Unlike our bolder, brasher American cousins, most of us would rather gnaw off our right arm than commit a social gaffe or be singled out for attention. A BBC television programme tested the traditional British abhorrence of 'making a fuss'. A series of secretly filmed experiments observed ordinary people's reactions to boorish behaviour by others. Actors shouted into mobile phones on trains, or smoked in non-smoking areas, or behaved in all manner of antisocial ways. In almost every situation, the people around them either tolerated the behaviour or silently sidled away. Asked afterwards why they had not said anything, some admitted fearing they would be punched on the nose, but most confessed they had simply been too embarrassed, reluctant to break the social convention not to make a fuss.

The programme's presenter, Adrian Chiles, though hardly a retiring wallflower himself, admitted that he had once spent a six-hour train journey watching a man continuously pick his nose, but could not bring himself to say anything.

A friend observed the following social rail crash.

Assassination on a train

A packed Southern Railways train is about to leave London's Victoria station heading for Brighton. Two teenage girls jump aboard at the last second. Squashed up against the door, they begin a loud, braying conversation which everyone on the carriage, though pretending to be engrossed in Su Doku, listens to intently. The girls engage in a major character assassination of a mutual friend called Tiggs, who they dismiss as being a thorough waste of space, obnoxious, man-mad, etc., etc. The train reaches Clapham Junction, where a large number of passengers get off, allowing the noisy pair to see across the carriage, to where an angry-looking girl of about the same age is sitting. 'Tiggs', exclaim both girls in unison, 'fancy seeing you here'.

Saying the wrong thing, at the wrong time and in the wrong place, is a classic recipe for embarrassment. Iowa-born writer Bill Bryson recalls the intense mortification he was caused as a child by his grandmother.

Politically incorrect sweet talk

During family visits to a local restaurant in Des Moines, Bill Bryson's grandma would habitually slip him a quarter and ask him to go out and buy some candy for later.

'And don't forget to get some NIGGER BABIES', she would shout as Bill walked out of the crowded restaurant. When he returned five minutes later, she would ask, in an equally loud voice: 'Did you remember to get some NIGGER BABIES? Because I sure love those ... NIGGER BABIES.'

'Grandma. You shouldn't say that', Bill would protest. 'They're called Liquorish Babies.'

The next week, at lunch in the same restaurant, Grandma handed Bill a quarter and megaphoned her instructions: 'Billy, go and get us some of those – whaddaya call 'em – LIQUORISH NIGGERS.'

Down the pub

Pubs, bars and other drinking holes present an interesting range of alcohol-laden embarrassment arenas. This is an uncomfortable world of spilled drinks, projectile vomiting, forgetting the punchline of tediously long jokes, overheated political and religious debates, transparent lies and bullshit, beer fights and karaoke.

Debbie Davies avoided all that, but still managed to embarrass herself.

The wrong pocket

Debbie was eighteen, and in the pub with some friends. Dungarees were fashionable back then in the eighties, and she was wearing her favourite pink pair. It had two pockets at the front. One contained a rolled-up five-pound note and the other a tampon.

When it came to her turn to buy a round, Debbie pulled the fiver from her pocket and waved it in the air, loudly declaring: 'This round's on me.' To her horror she realised she was in fact standing, like the Statue of Liberty, brandishing the tampon. All eyes in that crowded pub (and the entire world, it seemed) were upon her …

Perfect embarrassment is all to do with timing, and Debbie's was impeccable. But at least she lived to tell the tale.

Dead drunk

An inquest in February 1999 heard how a group of Sheffield pub regulars played a series of practical jokes on their friend, not realising he was no longer capable of seeing the funny side of things, indeed capable of anything.

Thirty-five-year-old Ian Clifton had passed out after drinking about eleven pints of lager and a quantity of home-made punch throughout the course of the day.

As he lay out cold in the pub, his friends shaved one side of his head and placed an inflatable doll on top of him which they photographed. The inquest heard that Ian had, by this time, been dead for about an hour, from acute alcoholic poisoning.

Jolly japes

Practical jokes, even when not being exercised on a corpse, can still be acutely embarrassing, sometimes for the perpetrator as well as the victim. The disc jockey from a US mid-west radio station may, on reflection, have regretted his little prank, played on listeners back in the 1980s.

Now you see it

The Iowa radio station presenter told his listeners that an Air Force Stealth fighter had landed at the little-used Mount Joy airport. More than 5,000 people turned up to take a look, but could see nothing. They began complaining to the radio station. The presenter told callers that the plane was there, but was shielded by a highly advanced cloaking device. To see it you had to 'move your head back and forth like a chicken and try to catch a glimpse out of the corner of your eye'. Police arriving at the scene were greeted by the sight of thousands of chicken impersonators. The DJ was suspended for two weeks.

I've never been caught trying to imitate a chicken in broad daylight, but have fallen for some of the oldest practical jokes in the book. Colleagues in a supermarket butcher's department once asked me to retrieve a 'long weight' for their meat-weighing machine, which had been loaned to a rival store further up the high street.

I arrived, explaining that John from Tesco had sent me for a long weight. 'Won't be a minute', I was told. 'Just take a seat.' The best part of an hour later, and bored senseless, the penny still hadn't dropped.

Or there was the time I was sent as a cub reporter on a local newspaper in Warwickshire to cover a story at the local Southam Zoo. The owner's wife had been bitten on the foot by a badger, I think. As I dashed out of the newsroom, the news editor handed me a folded piece of paper with the name of the person I should speak to. Arriving at the zoo, I retrieved the piece of paper, opened it and confidently asked the girl at the reception desk if I could speak to Mr G. Raffe.

There's one born every minute.

Party time

Although we are social creatures, this doesn't mean we're naturally gregarious or, indeed, party animals. Fear of embarrassment makes us shy. In extreme circumstances it causes crippling social phobia – but common or garden shyness is the more likely consequence. Shy people can still function fairly normally and are often quite comfortable about their condition, living happily within the restrictions it places upon them. But parties, as we shall see, are a real test.

In the UK, 60 per cent of the population experience shyness to some degree, according to the London Shyness Centre. In the US, 40–50 per cent of people describe themselves as being considerably shy. Self-confessed shrinking violets have included George VI, Jimi Hendrix, Wittgenstein, George Best, Laura Bush, David Beckham and Barbra Streisand.

Veteran trumpeter and broadcaster Humphrey Lyttelton once set fire to a vicar out of shyness. Lyttelton confesses that he had been a tremendously shy little boy, incapable of looking strangers in the eye. When his parents attempted to introduce him to a visiting vicar, young Humphrey rapidly dipped his head, accidentally butting the man in the stomach. The vicar burst into flames. It was nothing supernatural; a packet of Swan Vesta matches in his waistcoat pocket had ignited.

According to Kate Fox in her book *Watching the English*, shyness is quintessentially English.

> Shyness, diffidence or self-effacement have long been prized national traits. When it comes to self-introductions for example, one must appear self-conscious, stiff, ill at ease, awkward and, above all, embarrassed. Smoothness, glibness and confidence are inappropriate and un-English.

In party-land, even quite confident people can come unstuck.

Not a nibble

Midlands solicitor Paul Drew had not long embarked on his legal career when he accepted an invitation to a posh party to which he knew a number of legal luminaries had been invited. He arrived, cleaned and pressed, eager to impress – and hungry.

Looking anxiously around for someone to talk to, he reached out for what he took to be a bowl of fancy nibbles, scooped up a handful and shovelled them into his mouth. As he did so, his hostess approached with a senior member of the judiciary in tow. 'Hello Paul, I'd just like you to meet Judge …'

Which was the moment Paul realised that the bowl of nibbles he had tucked into was, in fact, potpourri. His attempt to make a good impression was slightly marred by his irresistible compulsion to cough rose petals, lavender leaves and cinnamon bark at the feet of his Honour, the learned judge.

Potpourri is not the only hazard to be overcome in social life.

I received a phone call one day from someone whose voice I didn't immediately recognise, but who embarked on a long and sad account of his recent misfortunes, including the fact that his wife had left him. After about ten minutes, I was intrigued but still mystified as to the identity of my caller.

Eventually he got to the point of his call. 'Anyway', he said. 'I'm pretty much over all that now, and am having a party, next Saturday, and hoped you and Di could make it.'

Now at this point I had the choice of a) making the embarrassing admission that I didn't know who I was talking to or b) missing a party. I chose embarrassment.

'This is terribly embarrassing', I began, 'but the truth is I have no idea who I'm talking to.'

'It's Tony, you idiot', he said. 'Tony Shew.'

'Of course it is', I stammered. 'This is a really bad line. I just didn't recognise your voice.'

'Never mind', he said. 'Just turn up at the party. It's fancy dress. Nothing too complicated, you just have to come dressed in pink. It's a Pink Party.'

We could manage that. Searching through our wardrobes, my wife and I managed to come up with a rather bizarre assortment of pink garments, including lycra cycling shorts, chiffon scarves, floppy hats and the like. Looking less than pretty in pink, we set off two days later for the party. Parking in a nearby side street, we hurriedly made our way to Tony's place, running a gauntlet of amused onlookers.

The house seemed oddly quiet as we approached. We knocked on the door, which was eventually answered by an astonished Tony in a dressing gown. We were a week early.

I wish I could say that that had been my most embarrassing party experience. It is, unfortunately, not. Many years earlier I had been invited to a party in Cardiff at the home of someone or other from BBC Wales. The comedian Max Boyce was there, and I think the rugby player Gareth Edwards. At some stage in the proceedings I noticed a man who seemed particularly worse for drink, staggering clumsily around, bumping into people, spilling their drinks. He wobbled over and slumped down on a sofa beside me. He was so drunk, even his eyes were rolling. 'Stop doing that with your eyes', I bellowed at him above the din of the music. I felt a tap on my shoulder and turned to see my host mouthing the words: 'HE'S BLIND.'

An actor friend tells me he once did something very similar with a dwarf. The rapper Busta Rhymes harangued a man in the front row of his concert for not getting up and dancing, until he realised he was in a wheelchair. Mark George did it with a bald woman.

No pleasure dome

Photographer's agent Mark George was invited to a cocktail party given by the firm of architects at which his father was a partner. Another of the partners had a rather beautiful Italian wife, Yvonne, whose good looks were slightly offset by her particularly thin hair, through which her scalp could quite clearly be seen.

When introduced to Yvonne, Mark couldn't take his eyes off her head. She asked him something, but he couldn't be quite sure what she'd said. In reality, she had asked him if he would like some food, but for some reason he was convinced that she had said: 'Do you think I'm bald?'

Mark, who is severely follically challenged himself, replied: 'No, no, no. Call yourself bald? No. You're not bald. Look at me, I'm bald.' Yvonne's startled reaction, and the intervention of other guests who tried desperately to change the subject, failed to divert him from his course, and he ploughed on relentlessly.

Until Yvonne's husband finally felled him with a blow to the solar plexus, probably.

It was rumoured amid New York literary society in the 1960s that the writer Ved Mehta, who wrote regularly in the *New Yorker* about his blindness, was not really blind at all. Some believed that his handicap was an elaborate literary hoax. The story goes that a literary editor once approached Mehta at a party and began sticking out his tongue and pulling faces to see if he would react. Unfortunately he was making a complete fool of himself in front of the perfectly sighted Nobel Prize-winning author V.S. Naipaul.

The Reverend Charles Dodgson (aka Lewis Carroll, creator of *Alice's Adventures in Wonderland*), loved children, though many biographers have suggested that his affection for little girls was not entirely healthy. For whatever reason, he was not one to turn down an invitation to entertain young people. Invited to one particular party, he avoided arriving a week early, but was less careful about checking the venue.

The bear unnecessaries

Lewis Carroll arrived at what he thought was a children's party and entered the parlour on his hands and knees, pretending to be a bear. Unfortunately, having misread the address, he found himself roaring around in front of an august gathering of feminist reformers.

'The embarrassed Carroll quickly rose to his feet', his nephew later recalled, 'and, without attempting any explanation, fled from the house.'

Two of the Marx Brothers managed to get both the date and the address right for a party, but not much else.

The wrong floor

Groucho and Harpo Marx were invited to a bachelor party at a restaurant in a posh hotel. The brothers had established that the elevator doors opened directly into the dining room and had prepared a surprise for their pals. Dressed only in top hats, with their clothes packed in suitcases, they burst out of the elevator with an expansive 'Ta Dah'.

To their acute embarrassment, they were greeted not by the expected roars of male laughter but by the high-pitched shrieks of a distinctly blushing bride and her friends, congregating in a dining room on another floor. They had pressed the wrong button.

The brothers, fearing the police would soon arrive, each grabbed a large potted plant, murmured apologies and backed out of the room.

Which reminds me of my uncle Arthur going into hysterics during a game of charades, trying to think of something to rhyme with the first word of the Marx Brothers' film *Duck Soup*. My grandmother guessed the title correctly just from my uncle's embarrassment.

Who am I?

Novelist Julian Barnes was in his early twenties when he was invited to his first literary party. He was very nervous and only managed some stumbling conversations with a few people before being introduced to Tom Maschler, the editorial boss of his publishers Jonathan Cape. He began to explain that he had contributed to a recent Cape anthology of ghost stories, but Maschler did not recall his name. 'What was the title of your story?' he asked.

A perfectly reasonable question, but it proved too difficult for the overawed Barnes, as he recalls:

> My mind was filled with a terrible blank. What the fuck was the title of my story? I knew it. I was sure I knew it. Come on, come on. You've just read the proofs. You've just written your own contributor's note. This is your publisher. You must know. It is impossible for you not to know.
> 'I can't remember', I replied.

And then there's the office party, about which I will do no more than quote American comedian Phyllis Diller, who said: 'What I don't like about office parties is having to look for a new job the next day.'

Dining out

Dinner parties involve a more formal etiquette than your common or garden party, or indeed your common garden party, and therefore offer more potential for social faux pas.

Publicly regurgitating your hostess's painstakingly prepared meal is not broadly recommended, though it does happen. George Bush Snr's re-presentation of a Japanese state banquet meal should not be cited as a precedent, even by presidents.

We should be on our best behaviour, chew our food properly and try to avoid insulting fellow guests.

Playing on my piano

During a dinner party held in his honour one evening, the Russian composer and pianist Sergei Rachmaninov mentioned his great affection for the Grieg piano concerto. His host, fellow pianist Arthur Rubinstein, revealed that he had, by chance, just recorded it. Rachmaninov insisted on hearing it, so Rubinstein fetched a copy of the recording and Rachmaninov, over coffee, closed his eyes and quietly listened.

The concerto over, he opened his eyes and offered his opinion: 'Piano', he observed, 'out of tune.'

Embarrassment can kick in even before you sit down to eat.

Putting your foot on it

US President Ronald Reagan was hosting a formal state dinner in honour of French President François Mitterrand. Protocol dictated that Nancy Reagan should lead Mitterrand to the table while her husband escorted Mitterrand's wife Danielle. Not as simple as it sounds, as President Reagan recalls:

> Nancy and François headed for their table, but Mrs Mitterrand stood frozen, even after a butler motioned at her that she was to walk toward our table. I whispered, 'We're supposed to go over there to the other side.' But she wouldn't move. She said something to me very quietly in French, which I didn't understand. Then she repeated it, and I shook my head. I still didn't know what she was saying; suddenly an interpreter ran up to us and said, 'She's telling you that you're standing on her gown!'

It's not usually done to tell your dinner hostess that her food is inedible, but newspaper columnist A.A. Gill actively encourages the practice. He once wrote a piece about sending back food at dinner parties. 'If it isn't any good', he suggested, 'ask your hostess to take it away and bring something else'. Years later he reflected that he still believed this was sound advice, though he had noticed that his dinner party invitations had somewhat dried up.

As a restaurant critic, Adrian Gill will have sent back food in some of the grandest of eating establishments. But most of us, even if we're paying through the nose for food not fit for pigs, are too embarrassed to complain. We will spend half an hour moaning among ourselves that the service is too slow, the food is cold, the meat overcooked and the vegetables taste of nothing. Then the waiter approaches and asks if everything is OK. 'Mmmm. Yes. Lovely thanks', we cowardly lie.

A recent survey, commissioned by the Devon-based Ashburton Cookery School, revealed that eating in a restaurant is a source of intimidation, embarrassment and shame. Nearly three-quarters of 200 young professionals questioned confessed that they wouldn't order dishes or drinks if there was a risk they might mispronounce the name. And 63 per cent said they would rather sit in silence than cause a scene by sending back unsatisfactory food.

And then there's the embarrassment associated with tipping. When should you tip, whom should you tip, and how much should you tip? And what's that 'discretionary' 15 per cent service charge all about? The travel editor of the *Independent*, Simon Calder, has spent a professional lifetime tiptoeing through the cultural minefield of gratuities. He has twice been chased down the street by waiters: once in New York after failing to leave a tip, and on the other occasion in Seoul where the waiter wanted to give him back his money. South Korea is one of a sadly diminishing number of countries where tipping is still occasionally considered an insult.

In the hairdressers, are you supposed to tip both the girl who washes your hair and the stylist, and if both, which should be given the bigger tip? I have wrestled with this one for years, and am still not sure if I've got it right. O, for those halcyon days in America when tipping was considered undemocratic and a public nuisance.

And a final tip for restaurant customers. Make sure you know the difference between the often confusingly stylised signs for male and female toilet facilities. I once spent a very uncomfortable half hour in a cubicle in the ladies' lavatory, waiting in vain for the place to empty so I could make my escape. Eventually, worried that my dining companions would think I had died, I coughed loudly and announced: 'Excuse me, I'm a man and I'm coming out.'

* * *

Food can be embarrassing even in less formal circumstances. Spinach, as we have already learned, terrifies teenage girls. Bananas, as we'll see later, are a menace to all and sundry. Author Douglas Adams had problems with biscuits.

Taking the biscuit

Douglas Adams went into a station cafeteria in America and bought a packet of cookies along with a newspaper, then sat at a table. A stranger sat down, opened the packet and started to eat them. There was obvious confusion and considerable embarrassment over the ownership of the cookies. 'I did what any red-blooded Englishman would do', said Adams. 'I ignored it.' Both men alternately removed biscuits from the bag until it was empty. It was only when the stranger left that Adams realised he had placed his newspaper over his own identical packet of cookies.

Norma Rowlerson had a little bit of bother with a muffin.

Having your cake

On a press trip to a skiing resort in Switzerland, travel journalist Norma Rowlerson was ready for a little lunch after a morning on the slopes. She helped herself to a cup of soup, a roll, some yoghurt and a muffin from the self-service counter. Sitting down, she decided she didn't really need the muffin, so discreetly slipped it inside her jacket for later.

She was then joined by her host, who put down his tray of food, before going back to get some cutlery. Looking down, Norma realised her muffin had slipped out of her jacket onto the floor. Checking that no one was looking, she scooped it up and returned it to its hiding place.

Her host returned, sat down, stared at his tray and said: 'Where's my muffin?' Norma, immediately realising what had happened, was faced with a dilemma.

'Most people would have denied all knowledge of the muffin', says Norma. 'I unzipped my jacket and handed over the thing. I don't remember what excuse I gave, but I know my face was bright red.'

Which wasn't quite the end of her embarrassment. As she left the restaurant after finishing her meal, her host called after her: 'If you ever need a muffin ...'

Across the border

Having established that the safest place to avoid embarrassment is in our own homes, it follows (sort of) that the further we stray from that safety zone, the greater the opportunity for embarrassment. And if we wander beyond our national boundaries we're really asking for trouble.

Embarrassment-free travel requires encyclopedic knowledge of world culture. We must know, for example, not to give somebody an even number of flowers in Romania, Russia, Slovakia, the Czech Republic, Hungary and Serbia – unless we're attending their funeral. We must know that the widely recognised gesture for OK, with the tips of first finger and thumb touching to form a rough circle, is taken to mean 'you're an arsehole' in Germany and Brazil. In many African countries we must be careful to avoid the right-handed handshake, and we should be aware that in Japan almost anything can contravene strict national codes of behaviour.

When I visited Japan to make a radio programme about the whaling industry, a Tokyo university lecturer kindly offered to act as interpreter for some interviews. Afterwards we went for dinner, where I ordered a bento box containing an assortment of delicious dishes, including a bowl of rice and some soy sauce. Knowing no better, I picked up my soy sauce and poured it over my rice. My translator gasped.

'What's wrong?' I said.

'Nothing', he replied. 'So sorry. I should not have reacted like that.'

The poor man was mortified, literally squirming in his seat. He could not look me in the eye. Eventually he explained that, in Japan (or at least in his neck of the woods), it was considered important to keep the rice separate from the soy sauce to preserve its purity of flavour and texture. I had inadvertently transgressed this sacred culinary rule. But he had committed a far greater crime, he believed, by demonstrating disapproval, particularly to an honoured visitor to his country. I looked hurriedly around to make sure there were no sharp knives within his reach.

If we survive the cultural clashes on our travels, we still have to cope with the language barrier.

Gained in translation

When the Parker company marketed a new ballpoint pen, their advertising posters were supposed to read: 'It won't leak in your pocket and embarrass you.' Unfortunately, the Spanish word *embarazar* was used by mistake to mean 'embarrass', when in fact it means something entirely different. The advertisement actually informed potential Mexican pen purchasers: 'It won't leak in your pocket and make you pregnant.'

Similarly, the Kentucky Fried Chicken slogan 'finger-lickin' good' came out in Chinese as 'eat your fingers off'. In the same line of business, American chicken farmer Frank Perdue used the slogan: 'It takes a tough man to make a tender chicken.' This appeared in billboards across Mexico as: 'It takes a hard man to make a chicken aroused.'

These kinds of embarrassing mistakes are made just as easily when foreign languages are translated into English. Many will be familiar to you, but here are a few corkers.

Cocktail bar in Norway: 'Ladies are requested not to have children in the bar.'

Doctor's office in Rome: 'Specialist in women and other diseases.'

Bar in Tokyo: 'Special cocktails for the ladies with nuts.'

Temple in Bangkok: 'It is forbidden to enter a woman even a foreigner if dressed as a man.'

Dental clinic in Hong Kong: 'Teeth extracted by the latest methodists.'

Hotel in Thailand: 'Please do not bring solicitors into your room.'

Hotel in Bucharest: 'The lift is being fixed for the next day. During that time we regret that you will be unbearable.'

Hotel in Paris: 'Please leave your values at the front desk.'

My language skills are embarrassingly bad. For years I used to back out of French shops or restaurants with a cheery '*bonjour*' to all and sundry, believing that 'good day' worked like the Italian '*ciao*'. The pitying looks on people's faces should have alerted me to my mistake long before the centime eventually dropped.

British Prime Minister Tony Blair would empathise. Appearing on the *Parkinson* television chat show, he recalled how he had once given a press conference in France and was asked if there was anything about French politics he particularly admired. Attempting to answer in French, Mr Blair replied: 'I desire your prime minister in many different positions.'

The French, though generally far superior to the British in language skills, can still get it terribly wrong.

Ride that pony

In 1995, French actor Olivier Martinez visited America to promote Jean-Paul Rappeneau's film *The Horseman on the Roof*, in which he was starring.

He spent two weeks telling the American public: 'I love to ride whores.'

'I didn't mean whores!' Martinez later explained. 'I wouldn't even know where to put the saddle ...'

* * *

Embarrassment lies in wait for all but the most hermit-like among us. Margaret Thatcher had it half-right. There is no such thing as society ... without embarrassment.

CHAPTER SIX

EMBARRASSMENT AT WORK

I had my heart set on a career in journalism.

A perfect opportunity arrived when I was just seventeen and was shortlisted for a place on the prestigious IPC journalist training programme, a two-year course which could end with a job on the *Daily Mirror* or one of the group's other newspapers. The selection process involved a weekend of tests and interviews.

Curiously, after all these years, I still remember a couple of the psychometric test questions. One was: 'Would you rather walk along a precipice or join a posse chasing a bandit?' Another simply asked: 'Do you like athletic men?' There was, mercifully, a 'Don't Know' option for most questions.

Afterwards came a series of interviews, the first with the deputy news editor of the *Daily Mirror*. He was a cartoon character of a newspaperman, with green eye-shade, red braces and intimidating bulk. Entering his office, I was invited to choose between a simple wooden chair and a newfangled, inflatable plastic thing. I thought: they're testing me, act cool, go for the plastic.

I lowered myself gingerly onto its cold, transparent surface, at which point it, more or less, ate me. I was sucked down into its yielding plastic innards, leaving only my feet protruding. I had to be hauled out by the news editor and his assistant. To this day I don't know if this was a deliberate practical joke or I had just been incredibly clumsy. I do know that I wanted to drop dead on the spot. I have no memory of the subsequent interview. Several weeks later I received a letter from IPC informing me that it had been decided to offer traineeships to the top six candidates. I had come seventh. If only I had plumped for the other chair.

Mark George, whom we met in the last chapter (upsetting a bald woman), also had problems getting selected for professional training. He rather fancied following in his father's footsteps and becoming an architect.

Hanging on the wire

Mark George was offered an interview for a place at architectural college. First, he and the other candidates had to complete a little test. They were each given a length of wire, and asked to fashion it into any shape they wanted.

Mark applied himself to the task and after much concentrated effort, came up with a nifty little rectangle. Raising it to eye level to check its geometry, he noticed that the candidate on his right had fashioned her piece of wire into the perfect likeness of a woman playing a cello. Mark correctly concluded that he was out of his league.

Work is where most of us manage to scrape together a little self-respect. A modestly successful career can compensate for our more general shortcomings as human beings. When things go well in our job, we feel cock-a-hoop, smug and self-satisfied.

Anyone doubting how important is the role that our job plays in maintaining self-esteem should try being made redundant. They say it's not personal, that they have been forced to make economies, to downsize, to *right*-size – but it feels damned personal. It feels like rejection. It is rejection.

But I'm over that now, honestly.

In a world which means the world to us, the smallest faux pas can seem like the end of the world.

> I've got some good news and some bad news. The bad news is that a lot of you have been made redundant. The good news is that I've been promoted.

Few of us will run into a boss quite as excruciatingly insensitive as the fictional David Brent in the BBC television series *The Office*. But most of us are more than capable of generating our own office embarrassment.

Penned in

Former New Zealand tennis player Brenda Perry was determined to make a success of her new role as a World Tennis Association tour director.

Chairing a meeting with a tournament director and several important sponsors, she was keen to present herself professionally. So it seemed like a disaster when, in the middle of trying to make a particular point, her hands moving around for emphasis, she somehow got her fountain pen tangled in her hair.

Despite subtle attempts to dislodge it, the pen remained stubbornly stuck. 'So I just left it hanging there', says Brenda, 'and no one in the meeting said a word or showed any reaction of any kind.' She finished

the meeting with the pen still in her hair and walked out
of the room summoning as much dignity as possible.

Most meetings, in my experience, are too long, too dull, and,
to be honest, utterly pointless; and I include the many meetings
I have chaired myself. A possible exception was the one where
I was chased terrified from a BBC department meeting by a
killer moth (honestly, it was huge), which was, at least, entertaining for everyone else.

Is there anything more irritating than failing to speak your
mind at a meeting for fear of embarrassment, only for a
colleague to achieve admiring comments for making exactly
your point? Blurting out 'That's just what I was going to say'
simply makes things worse.

And now back to our friend with the rectangular-shaped
piece of wire, for an imaginative way of achieving exquisite
embarrassment.

Jukebox fury

Having discarded his plans to become an architect,
Mark George settled into a career as a photographer's
agent.

In the early days Mark was quite nervous about dealing with the big advertising agencies. On this occasion,
in the flashy office of a senior art director at a leading
London agency, he handed over a portfolio of his
client's photographs and the director began to inspect
them by holding each transparency up to a skylight.

Mark paced back and forth, unsure whether or not
to say anything. He didn't want to seem pushy.
Distractedly he ambled over to inspect a large Wurlitzer
jukebox in the corner of the room, then folded his arms

and attempted to lean nonchalantly against the adjacent door frame.

But he leant a little too nonchalantly, slid down the wall and somehow managed to wedge himself into the dark and dusty space behind the jukebox, his nose pressed up against the skirting board.

After what seemed an eternity, Mark succeeded in wriggling himself free. But standing to face the art director, he found his padded jacket had ridden up and was now covering his head. This was not, he was sure, making a good impression.

After Mark eventually pulled his jacket down and himself together, he saw that the director was still working his way methodically through the photographs, apparently oblivious to his entire performance. Nothing was said, and Mark has never been quite sure exactly how big a fool he had made of himself.

Feel the burn

Matthew De Lange was working as a trainee accountant in the open-plan offices of Alcan (the foil people) in Chesham, Buckinghamshire.

It was in the days before computers, and Matthew had made a mistake in a column of figures. He pulled out a bottle of correction fluid but clumsily dropped a large blob of the liquid on his splendid new brown-striped suit trousers.

Undeterred, he got out a bottle of thinner, applied copious amounts to the crucial area and then carried on number crunching. Some minutes later the copious amounts of thinner, containing some fairly noxious chemicals, had soaked through his splendid brown-striped suit and his underpants and had arrived, burningly, at the more sensitive parts of his nether regions.

'My exit at speed through that open-plan office, grabbing my crotch and heading for the gents is still with me', says Matthew.

There are so many ways to embrace embarrassment at work. Slagging off the boss within his or her hearing will do it, or going to Newport on the Isle of Wight when your appointment is in Newport, Gwent, as a friend once did, or cutting your finger on a bacon-slicer and fainting on the first day of a new job. Backing out of a rather confrontational interview with some angry striking miners into a broom cupboard is another moment I have long struggled to erase from my memory.

I must also admit a catalogue of embarrassing mishaps during my days as a radio reporter and producer, involving tape recorders. I've lost count of the interviews I've done, only to discover that the pause button had remained on throughout. 'That was great', I would say, 'but I wonder if we could just run over a few of the main points again?' And once, recording a sitcom before an audience at the BBC's now demolished Pebble Mill studios, the cast had got halfway through their performance when I was informed that, because of a technical malfunction, nothing had been recorded. I had to stop proceedings, stand in front of the audience and explain that we had to start again, and would everyone please try to laugh just as enthusiastically as they had the first time around. And they did!

But I'm now going to make a clean breast of something I have never previously told a living soul. It's terrible – but the events happened nearly 25 years ago, so maybe I'm now safe from repercussions.

Working as a reporter for the Birmingham independent radio station, BRMB, I was regularly sent out in the radio car to cover stories. The vehicle had a large transmitter mast protruding from its roof, via which interviews could be beamed back to the newsroom. Returning the vehicle to its parking spot on this particular occasion, I failed to notice that the garage roller-gate had not been fully lifted, and succeeded in ripping the aerial from the top of the mast.

I examined the damage – which was severe. A combination of acute embarrassment and general cowardice drove me to try to cover up my crime. I jammed the aerial roughly back into its housing and covered the join with some masking tape. A puff of wind would have blown it off again. There was no way I was going to get away with this.

Back in the newsroom I handed the keys to a colleague who was waiting to take the radio car on another assignment. I got a cup of coffee and waited to be rumbled. Sure enough, he returned a few minutes later, but red-faced, confessing that he had driven the radio car into the shutter doors and snapped off the aerial. 'Never mind', I said. 'It could happen to anyone.'

And if you are reading this, Iain Webster – sorry.

Email hell

I was emailing an early chapter of this book to my publishers when I noticed that in the accompanying note I had inadvertently written 'losely' when I had meant 'loosely'. Too late, I'd pressed the 'send' button. I immediately fired off another email to reassure my editor that I was, in fact, perfectly aware of the correct spelling and was not completely illiterate.

A small slip, you might think, and hardly worth correcting in the circumstances. But it seemed important to me. How might I have reacted if I had been responsible for some of the following email horror stories?

Thank heavens I wasn't the government Transport Department spin doctor who sent out an email on September 11 suggesting it was a good day to bury bad transport figures. Jo Moore's insensitive communication triggered events which ultimately led not only to the loss of her job, but also that of her boss Martin Sixsmith and his boss, the Secretary of State for Transport, Stephen Byers.

More recently, former Tory parliamentary candidate Ellenor Bland was suspended from her party after she allegedly forwarded an email containing racist comments. Mrs Bland, a Wiltshire town councillor, claimed it had been her husband who had passed on the dubious material. 'I'm not a racist', she insisted – but expressed no opinion about her husband's behaviour.

An opera director (who wishes to remain anonymous) tells me how one of his productions nearly ground to a halt over a misdirected email.

A marriage not made in heaven

It's not unheard of for conductors and directors to clash, artistically, during the production of an opera. One particular young and ambitious conductor, embroiled in a variety of disputes with his director, petulantly detailed all his complaints in an email which he then sent to the entire cast and crew of the production of Mozart's *The Marriage of Figaro*.

The director, not wishing the argument to escalate, refrained from replying, but his production manager was incensed. 'What a precious little wanker he is', she wrote in an email intended, supportively, for the director's eyes only. Unfortunately she clicked 'reply' by mistake, and her comments flew through cyberspace to the conductor.

She received a curt 'Thank you' email back from the young maestro. Relations were frosty thereafter, but the production survived.

It's asking for trouble to write anything in an email that you wouldn't be happy to be seen by the world and his wife. Take, for example, the email which junior New York lawyer Jonas Blank intended solely for the eyes of his colleague Melissa, but ended up accidentally circulating to half the firm, including twenty of the partners.

I'm busy doing jack shit. Went to a nice 2hr sushi lunch today at Sushi Zen. Nice place. Spent the rest of the day typing e-mails and bullshitting with people. Unfortunately, I actually have work to do — I'm on some corp finance deal, under the global head of corp finance, which means I should really peruse these materials and not be a fuckup ...

So yeah, Corporate Love hasn't worn off yet ... But just give me time.

JLB

His angry bosses required young Jonas Blank to circulate a humiliating apology.

I am thoroughly and utterly ashamed and embarrassed not only by my behavior, but by the implicit reflection such behavior could have on the Firm. The content of the e-mail was inappropriate, showed a total lack of discretion, responsibility and judgment, and undoubtedly did my reputation and my future here no favors.

Although I cannot change what you and the other recipients saw, I do reiterate my sincerest apologies. I do and will take full responsibility for my actions in this incident, and I will do everything I possibly can to correct my mistakes and, more importantly, ensure that this and things like it will not happen again.

With sincere regret,

Jonas L. Blank

Emails can reach a wider-than-intended audience even without the sender's technical incompetence, once one or the other party decides to spread the news. A City lawyer's email row with his secretary over a £4 dry-cleaning bill made national news headlines in June 2005.

Taken to the cleaners

Richard Phillips, a senior associate with Baker & McKenzie, the world's fifth-largest law firm, emailed Jenny Amner asking her to foot the £4 bill for spilling tomato ketchup on his trousers. 'If you cd let me have the cash today, that wd be much appreciated', he wrote.

And Ms Amner replied on 3 June: 'With reference to the email below, I must apologise for not getting back to you straight away but due to my mother's sudden illness, death and funeral I have had more pressing issues than your £4. I apologise again for accidentally getting a few splashes of ketchup on your trousers. Obviously your financial need as a senior associate is greater than mine as a mere secretary.'

Ms Amner took the small extra step of copying details of the email exchange to her colleagues. From there the correspondence rapidly made its way around the globe. Recipients were divided on the merits of the case, some expressing sympathy for Mr Phillips, but most siding with Ms Amner.

Mr Phillips left his £150,000 job shortly afterwards, denying his departure had anything to do with the ketchup spat.

Emailers are well advised to follow the Green Cross embarrassment code and exercise extreme caution at all times. The safest thing is to leave the address field empty until you have finished typing your message, and then pause long and hard before deciding with whom you would wish to share details of your laziness, ignorance, criminality or sexual predilections.

Embarrassment on air

Radio and television can match email as a means of spreading mortification to the widest possible audience.

My short and inglorious career as a newsreader on the afore-mentioned BRMB radio station in Birmingham was littered with verbal gaffes, all committed in front of the second-largest commercial radio audience in England. My chronic inability to pronounce the word 'anaesthetist' once caused me considerable embarrassment, and on another occasion 'Tanzania' made me look a complete fool. At least I wasn't the local radio news-reader who, unaccountably, broadcast the following revelation.

'And now here's the latest on the Middle East crisis. Lesbian forces today attacked Israel. I beg your pardon. That should be Lesbanese ... I mean Lebanese forces ...'

One Saturday I took over news-reading duties from the station's news editor Brian Sheppard, who, before leaving the building, informed me that the next bulletin, at 1pm, should be three minutes long. Unfortunately he was badly mistaken. It was, in fact, scheduled to be a ten-minute bulletin.

Following orders, I prepared a brief bulletin – some headlines, a couple of short taped inserts and a weather forecast – and made my way to the news booth. The presenter on air at the time was Nicky Steele, who handed over to me on the hour before retiring to the toilet with a newspaper, expecting a decent break.

At the end of my three-minute bulletin I signed off: 'That's all for now. I'll be back with more news at two.' SILENCE.

'Well there seems to be time to look at some of those stories again', I stammered, and proceeded to repeat the entire bulletin.

Just as I was about to begin a third time, Nicky raced into his studio, put a record on the turntable and skipped into the newsroom for a few friendly words with me. He eventually calmed down enough to agree that the screw-up had been entirely the fault of the news editor. Dear old Brian Sheppard had, amazingly, done the exact same thing to Nicky the previous week.

Umpteen series of *It'll Be Alright On the Night* seem to prove that anything that can go wrong in the world of broadcasting will go wrong.

Not the news, at all

During the 2006 World Cup, BBC television news reader Natasha Kaplinsky announced live on air that Germany had been knocked out of the competition.

Kaplinsky, who had been flown out to Germany to co-anchor the Six O'Clock News, told viewers the 'big news' was that the host country had lost to Argentina. In fact, the two teams were still playing at the time – and Germany went on to win the game on penalties.

After making her critically flawed announcement, Kaplinsky paused briefly (presumably to receive a correction in her earpiece) and then went on: 'No I'm sorry, that is not the news at all.'

The embarrassment on that occasion was, presumably, shared between Miss Kaplinsky and whoever gave her the duff information in the first place. Newsreaders, generally speaking, don't make it up as they go along.

Sometimes broadcasters just get a bit too excited, as was the case when the BBC's John Simpson announced, back in November 2001, that he had liberated the Afghan capital, Kabul. Arriving in the city after the Taliban had fled in the face of Northern Alliance forces, Simpson announced: 'It's an exhilarating feeling to be liberating a city.' Afterwards he confessed to having got a bit carried away and said he was 'very, very, very embarrassed'.

Rabbi Lionel Blue, a veteran of BBC Radio 4's early morning *Thought For The Day* spot, was halfway through delivering one of his live three-minute scripts when he realised that the second page was missing. He had accidentally printed two copies of the first page. Momentarily flustered, he quickly composed himself and ploughed on, working from memory. It was a tricky moment, and he left the studio feeling he had made a complete fool of himself. To his surprise, and pleasure, he received hundreds of letters congratulating him on dealing so well with such an embarrassing situation. Without that unsolicited vote of confidence, he says he might have struggled to face the microphone again.

Broadcasting gaffes don't necessarily make it onto air ...

The wrong Maclean

Back in the early 1970s, Roy Plomley, the original presenter of the BBC's highly popular radio programme *Desert Island Discs*, was thrilled to learn that the famously retiring novelist, Alistair Maclean, had agreed to appear on the show and select his favourite eight records.

As was his habit, Plomley invited Maclean for a pre-recording lunch at the Savile Club in London.

They got on well, and after chatting for a while, Plomley asked Maclean who had most influenced his writing style.

'Oh, I'm not Alistair Maclean the writer', explained his lunch date. 'I'm in charge of the Ontario Tourist Bureau.'

It's rumoured that the BBC went ahead with the recording, rather than embarrass their Canadian guest. But the programme was never broadcast.

Novelist and broadcaster Jenni Mills recalls how an embarrassing gaffe more or less wrecked her television career.

Blood on the tracks

In the early 1980s, Jenni Mills was the presenter of a local current affairs programme broadcast by the Welsh independent television company HTV. On a train journey one day she fell into conversation with a fellow traveller who turned out to be a BBC television executive. Here was a chance to do a bit of networking, and perhaps advance her career prospects. On reflection she realises she may have been just a little indiscreet in her comments about her employers.

Back in the office the next day, the head of HTV current affairs strode up to her with a broad grin on his face. 'Ah, Jenni', he said. 'I hear you think I'm a dyed-in-the-wool news hack with very little creative imagination.' Her train conversation had been overheard by a third party who just happened to be her boss's best friend.

'He seemed to think it was all very amusing', says Jenni. 'But needless to say, my contract was not renewed at the end of the series.'

Jenni was intrigued by her ex-boss's reaction to her faux pas. 'He could have legitimately been embarrassed about the way I described him, but instead he chose to *hand the embarrassment over*, by confronting me with it', she says. Embarrassment leads to feelings of inferiority and weakness, but it's possible to gain a real sense of power by inflicting embarrassment on others.

One final confession from me before we leave the broadcasting arena.

I was making a radio series about a team of GPs in Lichfield, Staffordshire, and had been given permission to tape-record while surgeons carried out a routine hernia operation at a small local hospital. I assured everyone involved that I had been present at much more invasive and gory operations, so was unlikely to become squeamish during such a minor procedure.

But there was a difference. On the previous occasions I had been carrying a tape recorder and holding a large directional microphone. Somehow the technical paraphernalia had distanced me from the blood and guts of it all. This time the surgeon would be 'wired up' with a personal tape recorder and microphone and I was a mere observer. Come the first incision I hit the floor.

It was several days later that I listened back to the tape and heard the dull thud of my embarrassment, and the voice of the surgeon instructing his nurses to drag my unconscious body from the operating theatre.

The fine art of embarrassment

Imitation may be the sincerest form of flattery, but that's scant consolation if you've just forked out millions for a 'Picasso' daubed by a first-year art student. Art experts, dealers and collectors have long suffered both financial pain and personal humiliation at the hands of forgers.

Art forgery probably began with Roman sculptors producing copies of Greek statues, but it didn't take off in a big way until more modern times. After the Second World War, the British forger Tom Keating practised the forger's art on a grand scale, producing more than 2,000 fake paintings by 100 different artists, including Gainsborough, Rembrandt and Renoir. He claimed he did it not for financial gain, but to embarrass and destabilise a corrupt art world in which critics and dealers were 'lining their own pockets at the expense of naive collectors and impoverished artists'.

But others do it just for the money.

Away with the fairies

Fifty-four-year-old Robert Thwaites was a retired graphic designer with poor eyesight who took up painting as a hobby. Somehow he managed to fool a succession of art dealers and historians, including an art specialist from the BBC *Antiques Roadshow* pro-gramme, passing off forged paintings as the work of Victorian artist John Anster Fitzgerald.

The paintings, mainly of fairy scenes, were produced at Thwaites' home in Hertfordshire and sold for as much as £100,000 each. But scientific analysis eventually uncovered paint compounds which had not been available during Fitzgerald's lifetime. In September 2006, Thwaites pleaded guilty to the deception and was sentenced to two years in prison.

Art dealers and historians rarely admit to being embarrassed by their failure to spot forgeries. Their usual defence is to praise the extraordinary skill of the forger – in this case a former graphic designer with failing eyesight.

Experts at the Royal Academy appeared similarly unabashed by the suspect judgement they exercised while selecting artwork for their 2006 Summer Exhibition.

Head in the clouds

Visitors to the Royal Academy Summer Exhibition were invited to admire 'Exhibit 1201' – a small, roughly hewn piece of wood on an otherwise empty slate plinth.

But it wasn't supposed to be an exhibit. The artist David Hensel had merely intended it to support his actual work of art – a laughing head entitled *One Day Closer to Paradise*.

Somehow head and plinth had become separated. The art experts at the Royal Academy assessed them as separate works of art, and in their wisdom rejected the head and accepted the plinth.

The amused 64-year-old sculptor commented that 'some art critics should be boiled down to make soup for the homeless'.

A spokeswoman for the Royal Academy refused to admit that any error had been made on its part.

I have plans to submit an entirely blank canvas to the Royal Academy, calling it *Potential*. I'll let you know how I get on.

To be fair, it can be difficult to distinguish contemporary art from your elbow. Damien Hirst's *Painting-By-Numbers*, an installation comprising ashtrays, half-filled coffee cups and empty beer bottles, was scooped into a bin by a cleaner at the Eyestorm Gallery in west London in October 2001. The cleaner, Emmanuel Asare, said: 'It didn't look like art to me.'

You can't really blame him.

Publish and be embarrassed

Publishers, God bless them, can be as guilty as anyone of getting things embarrassingly wrong. Daniel Defoe's *Robinson Crusoe*, for example, was repeatedly rejected by a succession of publishing houses. William Thackeray couldn't get a publisher for *Vanity Fair*, so he published it himself in monthly instalments. The origin of 'vanity publishing'?

Step change

In 1977 Chuck Ross, a struggling writer, decided to try a little experiment to see how scrupulously publishers examine the manuscripts they receive. He typed up a fresh copy of Jerzy Kosinski's acclaimed novel, *Steps*, changed the title and submitted the work under his own name to fourteen publishers. All fourteen rejected the novel that had won the National Book Award in 1969 for best work of fiction. Among the publishers was Random House – the book's original publisher.

In October 2006, the academic publishers Duckworth were at the centre of a controversy over the veracity of one of their titles.

A bit of a fiddle

Among the Duckworth autumn books was an intriguing non-fiction work called *An Incomplete History of the Art of the Funerary Violin*. Written by Rohan Kriwaczek, it was described as 'a dark and magical history whose secrets will both fascinate and educate its readers'.

The book was full of impressive detail about the Guild of Funerary Violinists, whose motto *Nullus Funus Sine Fidula* means 'No Funeral Without a Fiddle', and of the great funerary purges of the 1830s and 40s, and about how funerary violinists duelled with each other to see who could wring the most tears from mourners.

But it soon emerged that there had never been any such thing as a funerary violin, that there were never any duels or any purges, and that the book was a work of total fiction – a hoax.

Duckworth's owner, the former Penguin boss Peter Mayer, reacted with a variation of the excuse used by art experts duped by forgers. 'If it is a hoax, it is a brilliant, brilliant hoax', he said.

Publicity surrounding the controversy was such that Mayer's company had to rush to reprint the book to meet public demand. Call me an old cynic, but I think I smell a rat here. Duckworth should certainly be embarrassed, but not, I suspect, for falling for a hoax; rather for their shameless publicity stunt. Apologies if I'm wrong.

The devil in the detail

That a book should be factually correct is obviously important, but it also needs to be free of printing errors. Too many errata are embarrassing. Not even the Bible has escaped, with various printing gaffes working their way into the holy scriptures down the centuries.

The 'Adulterous Bible' or 'Wicked Bible'
In 1631, the printers Barker and Lucas omitted the rather crucial 'not' from Exodus 20:14, making the seventh commandment read: 'Thou shalt commit adultery.' The printers were fined £300 and most of the copies were recalled. Only eleven copies are known to exist today.

The 'Sin On Bible', 1716
John 5:14 reads: 'Go and sin on more' rather than 'Go and sin no more'.

The 'Fools' Bible', 1763
Psalm 14:1 reads: 'the fool hath said in his heart there is a God', rather than 'there is no God'. The printers were fined £3,000 and all copies ordered to be destroyed.

And most aptly:

The 'Printers' Bible', 1702
Psalm 119:161 reads: 'Printers have persecuted me without cause.' The first word should have been 'Princes'.

Printing mistakes don't have to involve words – a simple punctuation error can do plenty of damage. Had Lynne Truss' invaluable book on the subject, *Eats, Shoots & Leaves*, been available in the 19th century, it might have saved the US government a lot of money.

Comma comedian

In the drafting of an important trade act, a US congressional clerk was supposed to write: 'All foreign fruit-plants are free from duty.'

Somehow he managed to transpose the hyphen into a comma, and it became: 'All foreign fruit, plants are free from duty.'

Before the mistake was spotted and a new act passed to correct it, the US Treasury had forfeited $2 million in taxes.

And punctuation mistakes can be monumental. Literary agent Charlie Viney tells of the unfortunate error on his uncle's tombstone. The epitaph was supposed to read 'King, Country, Music', but the engraver omitted the second comma.

But the real experts at both factual and printing errors are newspapers. The *Guardian*, appropriately renamed the *Grauniad* by *Private Eye*, is, by repute, the market leader in this respect, but it has plenty of competition from the rest of Britain's national and local press.

'Mrs Carson's husband, a garage proprietor, died almost two years ago in a road accident at Dornie Bridge. His condition last night was "satisfactory."'

Press and Journal, Dundee

'Charming blonde, Jean Harrington, plays Connie in the BBC1 series *All Creatures Great and Small*. Jean formerly played a secretary in *Crossroads* but she's recovered now and is acting again.'

Glasgow Evening Times

'The operation to trap the gang began on Friday when

a man arrived from Morocco on a car ferry. His car was followed to Prestwick where police ponced.'

Guardian

'Prince Philip's drive into Sydney was diverted at the last minute when a gelignite-and-nail bomb was found in a garbage can on the route. Another bomb was found at the central railway station. Police, who put an extra guard on the Prince, said: "We are dealing with a madman."'

Financial Times

'Mrs Barbara Stonehouse said last night that she was "absolutely delighted" that the Prime Minister's Commons statement had cleared her husband's name. It was the best thing that had happened to her family since her husband died ...'

The Scotsman

It's been happening since newspapers began, and all around the world.

Sideshow

Shortly before their marriage in December 1915, the US President Woodrow Wilson and his fiancée Mrs Edith Galt were spotted together watching a production at a local theatre. The *Washington Post* story the following morning was supposed to read that 'instead of paying attention to the play, the President spent the evening entertaining Mrs Galt'. Unfortunately the early editions of the paper accidentally suggested that Wilson had spent the time 'entering Mrs Galt'.

But apart from that, Mrs Galt, what did you think of the play?

Errors are sometimes, though not often enough perhaps, followed by contrite apologies (embarrassments in themselves), as in this example from the *Wilts and Gloucestershire Standard*.

Correction

'In our report of the visit last week of Health Secretary Patricia Hewitt to Cirencester, we described health cuts protestor, Ernest Knowles, 93, from Cirencester, as having two wooden legs.

'Mr Knowles has since pointed out that while he may be a little wobbly on his pins, they are still very much his own and he believes our reporter may have been misled by a joke made by his companion on that day.

'We apologise to Mr Knowles for any embarrassment our report caused him.'

Or this from *The Times*:

'Sir Max Aitken, former chairman of Beaverbrook Newspapers, was incorrectly described as the late Sir Max Aitken yesterday. We apologise for the error.'

Reports of the accuracy of newspaper reporting have been greatly exaggerated.

Please sir

My father, a primary-school teacher, never knew why the children in his class used to laugh when he banged his hand on his table to command their attention. I learned some years after his death, from one of his former pupils, that it was because it made the pollen fall out of the flowers he always kept there. They all found this hilarious. He would have been hugely embarrassed if he had known.

Children can be a tough audience, and it's the rare teacher who doesn't become the object of class ridicule from time to time. For some of the teachers at my old school it was an almost continuous experience, and we weren't a particularly difficult bunch. Francis Gilbert didn't call his best-selling classroom memoirs *I'm a Teacher, Get Me Out of Here* for nothing.

I don't like Mondays

Teacher Linda Quinn arrived at school on Monday morning a little the worse for wear. She'd been celebrating a friend's birthday the previous evening, overslept and rushed out of the house in a bit of a hurry. Her class of fourteen-year-olds was waiting for her.

'I walked in calmly and proceeded with the music lesson as if everything was normal', she says. Despite a shocking hangover she managed to get through the lesson, but noticed that there was an unusual amount of sniggering going on among her pupils.

It wasn't until she was about to leave at the end of the day that she finally noticed that the dress she was wearing was not just back to front, but also inside out. 'The label was clearly visible at my neck, and threads hung down at the waist and hem', says Linda. 'No wonder everyone was laughing.'

The headmaster involved in this next story revealed a lot more than Linda, but was probably less embarrassed.

Dangling conversation piece

Paul was twelve and a prefect at his preparatory school. It was his final day before leaving for Eton, and the elderly headmaster, a man more feared than revered, called all the prefects together for a final little chat.

'As you travel on through life you will be expected to behave like men', he told them. 'This will include some business with women.'

Just as Paul and his friends were beginning to wonder what he was driving it, all was revealed. The headmaster dropped his trousers and pants, exposed his aged manhood and announced: 'This is what yours will look like when the time comes, boys. You need to be prepared.'

No, it was not Baden Powell.

Paul (not his real name) tells me he doesn't recall being particularly embarrassed by the experience. Worse things happened at preparatory school apparently – and at Eton.

Then there's the teacher who experienced such acute embarrassment that she felt the need to seek recourse from the courts.

The embarrassing chair

Deputy headmistress Sue Storer attempted to sue her local education authority for £1.5 million, claiming she was forced out of her job by a chair that made a farting sound whenever she sat in it. The 48-year-old mother of two told an employment tribunal that the rude noise embarrassed her in front of children, parents and fellow staff.

She said: 'It was a regular joke that my chair would make these farting sounds. I regularly had to apologise that it wasn't me, it was my chair.' Her demands for a replacement had, she complained, been snubbed.

The farting chair was, she alleged, typical of the sexist way she was treated at the school. The learned tribunal turned down her claim for constructive dismissal, taking the not unreasonable view that she could easily have organised a new chair for herself.

Perhaps a kind teacher could offer her a handkerchief to dry her tears. Tony Hammond, perhaps?

Underwear aware

Tony Hammond, an English teacher at St Paul's School in London, was trying to engage his class of adolescent pupils in the attractions of *As You Like It*.

Pulling out his handkerchief to blow his nose, he found himself wafting a pair of his wife's knickers in front of the class. Aghast, he quickly thrust them back in his pocket before, he thinks, anyone had noticed. He still shudders at the thought of the years of ridicule which were so narrowly averted.

Holy disorders

Having survived a career as a schoolteacher relatively unscathed, Tony Hammond retrained as a rabbi. To date he has succeeded in controlling the impulse to wave his wife's underwear at his south London congregation, but has found other routes to embarrassment.

Dearly departed

Conducting his first funeral service, Rabbi Tony

Hammond became momentarily confused between the Hebrew word for the prayer for the dead (*Kaddish*) and that for a wedding blessing (*Kiddush*).

He carried on and made it through the ceremony, despite being horribly distracted by the thought that he had very possibly committed a highly embarrassing gaffe. Had he said *Kaddish* or *Kiddush*?

Afterwards a congregant discreetly informed him that he had in fact asked the funeral mourners to recite the wedding blessing.

The synagogue, like the church, mosque or temple, offers no sanctuary from embarrassment. The Revd Dick Lucas will never be allowed to forget his unfortunate faux pas in the pulpit.

On the record

Returning to work after a period of ill health, Dick Lucas, the long-serving curate of St Helen's Church in Bishopsgate, London, got up to deliver his sermon, dressed in his trademark cardigan.

He began: 'I feel I have hardly begun to understand how to teach the Bible to the world in which we live today.'

So far so good. But he went on to say: 'And sometimes when I have stood in the pulpit, when I've just been praying to myself as the hymn is being sung before the sermon, I've said: Lord, you've got a dead Dick on your hands this morning. Please revive me.'

Which he might have got away with, if some kind member of the congregation hadn't tape-recorded it and posted it on the Christian website Ship of Fools.

Nobody was recording the following sermon, but the Archbishop of Armagh has openly confessed his embarrassment.

Out of the mouths of babes

The Archbishop of Armagh was preaching one Sunday, at the first service after a new stained-glass window had been installed in the church.

Wanting to involve the younger members of the congregation in his sermon, he asked if any of the children could say what was different about the church, compared with the previous Sunday.

There was a long silence and then a little hand in the back row was raised and a confident voice called out: 'Please sir, there aren't as many people here as there were last Sunday.'

And perhaps we should spare the Rt Revd Dr Tom Butler further humiliation following his late-night antics back in November 2006, which included throwing children's toys from a car, crying: 'I'm the Bishop of Southwark. It's what I do.' He said at the time that it would be 'out of character' for him to have been drunk. But we all act out of character from time to time, do we not?

The thin blue line

Where are our wonderful policemen when we really need them, to tell us the time or give us directions to the pub? Out chasing murderers and thieves and other such nonsense, no doubt. In fact, most of the time the police do a marvellous job, keeping our streets safe enough for you and I to stand around complaining about them. But every now and again, of course, like everyone else, they get it embarrassingly wrong.

It's a steal

Manchester plumber John Curley was distinctly unimpressed by his local constabulary's handling of a theft from his van.

A thief had broken the vehicle's window and was removing hundreds of pounds worth of tools when he was spotted by Mr Curley's neighbour, who immediately dialled the police on his mobile phone.

With the police listening in, the neighbour confronted the young miscreant, who responded by claiming he was Mr Curley's nephew and was removing his uncle's tools for safe keeping. He then brazenly asked to speak to the police personally, and proceeded to repeat his story.

Instead of rushing to investigate, as the neighbour had requested, the police accepted the man's story and even offered to send round a police car to assist him, The man declined their kind offer.

David Blunkett, a man perfectly capable of embarrassing behaviour of his own, was once at the centre of an unfortunate police blunder.

The Blunkett file

As a high-profile terrorist target, Home Secretary David Blunkett had every reason to expect total vigilance from the police officers responsible for guarding his safety. So he was probably not too impressed when he learned that a confidential police file containing all his security details had been mislaid.

The dossier contained aerial photographs of Mr Blunkett's home in Sheffield, details of his alarm system and a list of places he frequently visited. It was eventually discovered lying in the street outside a pub, just yards from a Sheffield police station.

Head of South Yorkshire police, Mike Hedges, was called in for a 'chat' with Mr Blunkett, and afterwards said he was 'very embarrassed' and that he wanted to make sure such a security lapse never happened again.

Security leaks can be very serious, but it was a different kind of leak which cost a senior police officer his job back in February 2002.

Wet on the wall

Chief Superintendent Kevin Pitt admitted that he was guilty of 'a grave error of judgement which has caused embarrassment to me, my family and Cleveland Police'.

Chief Supt Pitt's crime? He was caught on CCTV urinating against the wall of the Presidential Palace in the Lithuanian capital of Vilnius, while on a visit to the country to advise on training of anti-corruption investigators.

Resigning from the police after 30 years' service, he added that it was the 'only honourable option' considering his behaviour.

Even G-men are fallible.

Bit of a giveaway

Top FBI undercover agent Tom Bishop (not his real name) was famed for his skill at assuming false identities in high-risk situations. On one occasion he flew to Dublin posing as a crooked art collector looking to buy some stolen paintings from the notorious gangster Martin Cahill.

To convince the Cahill gang he was genuine, he handed over an envelope containing photos allegedly of his own collection of stolen art (in fact, artworks that the FBI had previously recovered). As the gang leafed through the photos, one of them pulled out a piece of paper from the file. On FBI headed notepaper it read: 'Tom, don't forget these ...'

The law is an ass

Once the police have nabbed their man (or woman) and brought him (or her) before the courts, there are still plenty of things that can go horribly wrong. The judicial system and its practitioners are neither above the law nor beyond embarrassment.

Travesty of justice

In September 2005, a judge threw a rape case out of court on the simple grounds that there was absolutely no forensic, medical or identification evidence linking the defendant to the offence. Judge Roger Saunders said the barrister, Justin Bearman, who had advised the police and Crown Prosecution Service to charge the man, had been talking 'utter rubbish' and should personally pay the costs of the prosecution.

Not that judges are perfect in every possible way, of course, in or out of the courtroom. We've already considered US Judge Donald D. Thompson and his penis pump, but he's by no means the only member of the judiciary to have attracted embarrassing headlines in relation to sexual goings-on.

Hot enough to blow your wig off

In the autumn of 2006, 60-year-old British immigration judge Mohammed Ilyas Khan found himself the central player in a tale of sex, blackmail, explicit videos, cocaine, and torrid emails in which he called his illegal immigrant Brazilian cleaner Roselane Driza 'chilli hot stuff' in bed. Both Judge Khan and a female immigration judge embroiled in the saga had employed Driza while she had no legal work permit.

Leading QC David Pannick argued at the time that little would be achieved by a formal inquiry into the judges' behaviour. 'Not all judges have good judgement', he wrote in his regular column in *The Times*. 'And there is no fool like an old fool.'

David Pannick knows a thing or two about the way the law, and those who practise it, can be made to look an ass. He produces an annual review of the legal world's less judicious moments – and 2005 would seem to have been a vintage year.

His award for 'least judicious judge of the year' went to Franklin Jones of New Hampshire, who resigned after groping five women at a conference on sexual assault and domestic violence.

And he had a number of contenders for the most absurd lawsuit.

- Pop star Bono, who successfully sued his former stylist in a Dublin court for the return of a pair of trousers and a hat that he insisted had 'iconic status'.
- A prisoner in Romania who was suing God for failing to save him from the Devil, in breach of the contract made at the time of his baptism.
- A woman in Brazil claiming damages from her partner for failing to give her orgasms.

- A legal dispute in which the radical Muslim preacher Abu Hamza refused to leave his cell to attend a preliminary hearing of criminal charges because of a disagreement over the length of his toenails.

But the award for the most absurd lawsuit of 2005 went to:

- Marina Bai, an astrologer, who was suing the US space agency NASA in a Moscow court for £172 million for launching a space probe into a comet, thereby, she alleges, 'distorting my horoscopes'.

In the US, several successful books have catalogued some of the wonderfully embarrassing moments which arise during courtroom testimony and cross-examination. The following is a classic, and allegedly genuine example.

ATTORNEY: Doctor, before you performed the autopsy, did you check for a pulse?

DOCTOR: No.

ATTORNEY Did you check for blood pressure?

DOCTOR: No.

ATTORNEY: Did you check for breathing?

DOCTOR: No.

ATTORNEY: So, then is it possible that the patient was alive when you began the autopsy?

DOCTOR: No.

ATTORNEY: How can you be so sure, doctor?

DOCTOR: Because his brain was sitting in a jar on my desk.

ATTORNEY: But could the patient have still been alive nevertheless?

DOCTOR: Yes, it is possible that he could have been alive and practising law somewhere.

The late Judge Harrison-Hall was a popular member of the judiciary, esteemed for his wit as much as his judgement. But he's also remembered for committing what appeared to be an unfortunate gaffe during one particular case before him.

It's all about timing

It was a couple of days into a trial at Warwick Crown Court in which a man charged with rape was appearing before Judge Harrison-Hall.

The complainant was in the witness box, giving evidence about the circumstances leading up to the alleged offence. It was fast approaching lunchtime as the girl began to describe the sexual assault. 'He took out his penis', she told the court. 'And stuck it in me.'

At which point Judge Harrison-Hall interrupted, saying: 'Yes, and it's one o'clock, so we had better leave it there until after lunch.'

Was this an embarrassing faux pas by the learned judge, or had he mischievously, and slightly inappropriately one might think, said it on purpose? The jury's still out on that one.

The business of embarrassment

Dick Rowe, the A&R man at Decca records, committed what is probably the greatest blunder in the history of the music industry, turning down the chance to sign The Beatles because he thought guitar groups were on their way out.

He does, however, have competition.

It's for you

In 1876, William Orton, president of the Western Union Telegraph Company, was approached by Alexander

Graham Bell and offered exclusive rights to his new invention, the telephone, for $100,000. Orton is reported to have turned Bell down flat, dismissing his creation as 'an expensive toy with too many design faults'.

Orton soon realised his mistake and tried to launch his own telephone system. Bell immediately sued for infringement of copyright and defeated Western Union in the courts. Orton's business myopia had resulted in what is generally considered to be the worst business decision in the history of the United States.

Once you have a good product, it's necessary to draw attention to its virtues. Here, again, things can go embarrassingly wrong. Who, for example, was the genius who came up with the slogan used by the Scandinavian vacuum manufacturer Electrolux, when it first tried to sell its goods in the US: 'Nothing sucks like an Electrolux'? For some reason this didn't seem to impress the American public.

The world's most successful businessmen demonstrate a range of qualities: a brilliant command of the marketplace, a ruthless streak as long as your arm, and the ability to avoid saying and doing the wrong things. Gerald Ratner's famously embarrassing admission that his company's jewellery was 'crap' was most definitely a wrong thing. And he had plenty of time to consider his mistake while clearing his desk.

Good judgement is equally important for bosses of public utilities.

Clever Trevor

Yorkshire Water chief executive Trevor Newton lived to regret telling the world he had stopped taking baths or showers.

His 'admission' came during the drought of 1995. He was trying to stress the importance of conserving water, by demonstrating how frugal he and his wife were being at home.

'I personally haven't had a bath or shower for three months', he told a press conference. 'And no one has noticed.'

But it was subsequently revealed that Newton, whose company was already highly unpopular for making excessive profits, had been slipping out of the area to have a 'stealth bath' at his mother's house.

The newspapers showed no mercy.

Making money on the stock market is easy. You just buy low and sell high. Nothing to it. But it does require a shrewd grasp of market trends, or at least some reliable advice from the experts. But sometimes they can get it catastrophically wrong.

A perfect time to invest

On 16 October 1929 the eminent economist Irving Fisher made an announcement: 'Stock prices have reached what looks like a permanently high plateau ... I expect to see the stock market a good deal higher than it is today within a few months.'

Nine days later he was forced to eat his words, when $3 billion in stock values were wiped out in just one hour of trading. It was the start of the devastating Wall Street Crash.

Fisher wasn't the only person to fail to see the writing on the wall. The day after the Crash began, at least one national newspaper was still announcing: 'Bankers Optimistic.'

Bankers didn't get their entry into Cockney rhyming slang for nothing.

The embarrassment of riches

Those of you who don't have too many brass farthings to rub together may find this hard to accept, but it's not always easy being rich.

Comedy writer and actor Ricky Gervais admitted that the US television networks virtually threw cash at him after *The Office* collected two Golden Globes. 'The money being offered was criminal', he said. 'It's embarrassing enough being an actor for a living – it's a worthless job – but when people know you earn a thousand times what a nurse earns, it's fucking embarrassing.'

Paul Newman, having made a considerable amount of money from his film career, decided he wanted to 'give something back', so he started a company, Newman's Own, selling salad dressing and other food products. He turned it into a multi-million pound enterprise, which every year donates all its profits to charity.

Newman's generosity appears to have been motivated by genuine altruism, a deep-felt need to share his good fortune. I'm sure this is also what has driven hugely successful businessmen and financiers like Richard Branson, George Soros, Bill Gates and Warren Buffett to pour billions into charitable causes. All these men, to some extent or other, have grown embarrassed by their wealth. Their generosity makes them feel better about themselves. It's human nature.

Some of the great philanthropists of earlier centuries were probably giving away their money in order to save their immortal souls. They were often more embarrassed about the way they acquired their fortunes than they were about the money itself.

Andrew Carnegie, a Scottish emigrant to the US, made his fortune from steel. He wrote 'the man who dies rich, dies disgraced'. He had given away his entire $350 million fortune by his death. During his life he had made his steelmen work twelve-hour days, seven days a week, and brutally suppressed strikes among the workforce. 'Maybe with the giving away of his money', commented his biographer Joseph Wall, 'he would justify what he had done to get that money'.

Similar contradictions occurred among British philanthropists, like the York chocolate manufacturer Joseph Rowntree. He contributed generously to a whole raft of philanthropic concerns, including anti-slavery and temperance movements. In business he stole trade secrets, dismissed women employees upon marriage, and let go young men at the age of 21 when they became too expensive.

These men didn't have to give all their money away. For that we must thank the embarrassment of riches.

A week is a long time

Politics is the art of looking for trouble, finding it everywhere, diagnosing it incorrectly and applying the wrong remedies.

Groucho Marx

Embarrassment always involves a 'perceived diminution of public esteem'. For a group of people already held in such low esteem (invariably bottom in opinion polls of the nation's most trusted people), politicians might be expected to be impervious to the emotion.

And yet embarrassment can be fatal in politics.

Being conspicuously sweaty did for Richard Nixon. Being caught in a lie finished off Stephen Byers. Sexual indiscretion was an embarrassment too far for John Profumo, Welsh Secretary of State Ron Davies, and Lib-Dem leadership contender Mark Oaten. Neil Kinnock's triumphalism at a Labour rally just prior to the 1992 general election is widely believed to have cost him victory. Peter Mandelson, David Blunkett, Iain Duncan Smith and many others like them, from all shades of the political spectrum, became just too embarrassing for their parties and were required to fall on their swords.

Other politicians survive their embarrassing moments but remain scarred by the experience. Tony Blair may have come to terms with his loss of popularity over the Iraq war, but will never live down being roundly booed by the Women's Institute.

All politicians are easy and, indeed, legitimate targets for the slings and arrows of outrageous journalists, satirists, cartoonists and other critics from both inside and outside their own parties.

'He is undoubtedly living proof that a pig's bladder on a stick can be elected as a member of Parliament.'
Labour MP Tony Banks on Tory MP Terry Dicks

'Begotten of froth out of foam.'
Herbert Asquith on Winston Churchill

'Richard Nixon is a pubic hair in the teeth of America.'
Graffiti

'A triumph of the embalmer's art.'
Gore Vidal on Ronald Reagan

The politician who wants to steer clear of serious scorn doesn't necessarily have to possess huge intellect, dazzling wit or even charisma. He or she simply has to avoid appearing ignorant. It's amazing how many fail to achieve this.

On being appointed Sports Minister after Labour's 2001 general election victory, Richard Caborn foolishly agreed to have his sporting knowledge tested live on the radio. The questions wouldn't have taxed the average schoolboy, but poor old Richard didn't get a single one right.

George W. Bush has never given the impression that he's an intellectual giant. He may be hiding his light under a bushel, but it's an awfully big bushel. Once, when asked by a journalist if he could name the president of Chechnya, he replied: 'No. Can you?' Well how about the prime minister of India? 'The new prime minister of India is … er … er … no.'

Ronald Reagan might also have struggled in a quiz about world leaders (didn't he think Valéry Giscard d'Estaing was a woman?), but, with his actor's instincts, would probably have avoided this excruciatingly embarrassing exchange between Bush and a blind reporter from the *Los Angeles Times*.

GEORGE W. BUSH: Peter. Are you going to ask that question with shades on?
PETER WALLSTEN: I can take them off.
BUSH: I'm interested in the shade look, seriously.
WALLSTEN: All right, I'll keep it, then.
BUSH: For the viewers, there's no sun.
WALLSTEN: I guess it depends on your perspective.
BUSH: Touché.

Gerald Ford was another president not famed for his intellectual prowess. 'There's nothing wrong with Gerry Ford', Lyndon Johnson is supposed to have remarked, 'except that he played football too long without a helmet'. More famously he observed: 'Gerry Ford can't fart and chew gum at the same time.'

Ford's clumsiness also caused him embarrassment; famously

falling down the steps of Air Force One and cartwheeling down ski slopes. He didn't have much more luck on the golf course, gaining a reputation for hitting more spectators than fairways. Bob Hope once joked: 'It's not hard to find Gerry Ford on a golf course – you just follow the wounded.'

Democrat presidents also have their bad days.

Carter and the killer rabbit

Jimmy Carter's re-election campaign received a bit of a setback in April 1979 when he was attacked by a swimming rabbit while fishing from a small boat on a lake in Plains, Georgia. The rabbit, from a distance, seemed to be trying to board the President's boat, but swam off after Carter flailed at it with a paddle.

Photographs of the proceedings found their way onto the front page of the *Washington Post* under the head-line PRESIDENT ATTACKED BY RABBIT. The incident was even turned into a song by Tom Paxton, with the lyrics 'I don't want a bunny wunny in my little rowboat'.

At least, for Carter, it made a change from jokes about peanuts.

This next story was reported in the *New York Times* in October 2000.

Like a candle in the wind

German Chancellor Gerhard Schröder, attending a solemn ceremony at Jerusalem's Yad Vashem Holocaust Memorial, was invited to turn a handle to boost the eternal flame commemorating the death of millions of Jews during the Holocaust.

To the acute embarrassment of everyone present, the

Chancellor turned the handle in the wrong direction, and extinguished the flame. The Israeli Prime Minister, Ehud Barak, stepped forward and tried to help, but it took a technician (with a butane lighter) to put things right.

Meanwhile, in the land of the midnight sun ...

War games

In January 2003, a Norwegian member of parliament was spied on camera playing war games on his pocket computer while colleagues debated the possibility of real war in Iraq.

Trond Helleland of the ruling Conservative Party had, apparently, been unable to resist the temptation to try out a new game, *Metalion*, after checking his electronic diary for appointments. He played the game for about seven minutes without realising that television crews had zoomed in on him and would later feature the footage on the national news.

'I realise it was very stupid of me', he admitted afterwards. 'I will not do it again.'

My most embarrassing encounter with a politician happened in Bangladesh when I went with BBC correspondent Alex Kirby to interview the country's environment minister, Mrs Chowdhury, about the impact of climate change. As requested, I'd faxed a list of questions in advance.

Unaware that her aides had provided her with a list of answers carefully typed on a series of numbered cards, Alex began asking the questions in a different order. But Mrs Chowdhury gave her answers in the order she had expected the questions. It was like a *Two Ronnies* sketch. Her embarrassed assistant fluttered around her, desperately trying to match the cards to the questions. Eventually Mrs Chowdhury resolved the matter by throwing down the cards and addressing the questions directly. She gave an immaculate interview.

I know this next story sounds very much like a joke, but it comes from an impeccable source: the historian Geoffrey Moorhouse in his book *The Diplomats*.

All I want for Christmas

It was Christmas Eve, 1948, and a Washington radio station was telephoning ambassadors from various countries to ask what they would wish for at this festive time of year.

'World peace', replied the French ambassador. 'Justice for all oppressed people', suggested his Russian counterpart. Other ambassadors wanted an end to poverty or a moratorium on nuclear testing.

Next came the British ambassador, Sir Oliver Franks. 'Well, it's very kind of you to ask', he said. 'I'd quite like a box of crystallised fruit.'

I can't find a historian who can corroborate this next story, but the website from which it's borrowed insists that it's true. I do hope so.

I've fallen in the water

While visiting an air-force base, the Greek dictator General Metaxas was invited to test a new flying boat. After a short flight, he was approaching a runway to land when it was respectfully pointed out to him that it might be better to come down on water as it was a flying *boat*.

The General pulled up, made another pass, and safely touched down on the water. After killing the engine he turned to his co-pilot and said: 'Thank you for saving me from making a fool of myself' – before opening the craft's door and jumping out into the water.

Embarrassment is such damned hard stuff to erase. For a politician, a lifetime of selfless devotion to public service can be wiped out by a moment's indiscretion. Whatever line of work we're in, there's always a risk that we'll be remembered for our weaknesses rather than our strengths, our verbal slips rather than our bons mots, our moments of madness rather than our years of dedicated professionalism.

If only it were possible to reach back in time and snatch back our embarrassing moments.

In the case of embarrassing emails, it was rumoured back in 2003 that Microsoft had developed the technology to allow us to destroy messages by remote control, even after they had arrived in their recipient's mailbox. Alas it was a myth.

Embarrassment, electronic or otherwise, like mud, sticks.

CHAPTER SEVEN

IN THE SPOTLIGHT

All the world's a stage, and all the men and women merely players.

William Shakespeare

On the great, metaphorical stage of life we still get to choose whether we want to be a leading actor or a spear-carrier; whether we want to conduct our lives centre stage or to hover inconspicuously around the wings or in the chorus line. Staying in the chorus line keeps us out of the embarrassment firing line and avoids any risk of attracting unfavourable reviews.

In this chapter we're concerned with people who choose to put themselves literally on the stage, or at least to perform in one way or another. It might be anything from third shepherd in a school nativity play to the starring role in a Hollywood blockbuster, from telling a joke at an office party to baring one's soul (and pretty much everything else) in a reality TV programme. Each activity requires us to step out of the shadows and into the spotlight – and to be prepared to risk the consequences. In all cases the likelihood of embarrassment is alarmingly high.

Noël Coward understood the perils of appearing on the

stage, and tried to dissuade Mrs Worthington from exposing his daughter to them. But for the constraints of chronology, he might have told her what once happened to *All Creatures Great and Small* star, Christopher Timothy.

Oh Timothy

In the 1960s, Christopher Timothy's acting career amounted to little more than playing small walk-on parts on stage. But he did get the exciting opportunity to bring his spear-carrying expertise to the services of the great Laurence Olivier in a National Theatre production of *Othello* at the Old Vic. Things went swimmingly until the night he became over-engrossed in a game of Scrabble in his dressing room and missed his cue for the famous carousing scene in Act II. Realising his mistake, he did what any actor would do in the situation – he panicked, grabbed his wig and rushed to the stage.

Christopher was supposed to be a member of a crowd singing and fighting in a drunken brawl. He arrived in the wings, picked up the one remaining goblet from the props table, and making loud 'I'm extremely drunk' noises, staggered onto the stage – where he found that his scene was over and the only people there, in a very quiet, intimate scene, were Laurence Olivier (Othello) and Maggie Smith (Desdemona).

Exit stage right, pursued by embarrassment.

We don't all want to see our names in lights, but few of us would wish to live our lives in total anonymity. And it's nice to think we might leave some sort of faint smudge in the sands of time. But those who achieve any kind of lasting fame or celebrity are simply opening themselves up to a potential myriad of new and unpredictable forms of humiliation.

Stephen Rhodes' mortification came, not in front of the whole world, but at least a thousand people.

Behind you

Midlands radio presenter Stephen Rhodes had been hired to entertain the Birmingham Hippodrome audience during the interval of the Christmas pantomime production.

While the cast was in the bar getting fortified for the second half, Stephen brought half a dozen kids on to the stage, chatted to them about the show and then sent five of them back to their seats with a gift. The last child, a cherubic little boy of about six, he pretended to forget.

Stephen carried on talking to the audience with his back to the boy, expecting the little tyke to tug at his jacket and display childish indignation. Instead he just dissolved quietly and heartbreakingly into floods of tears. The audience, aghast, were shouting something to the effect of 'he's behind you', but Stephen, assuming they were joining in the joke, remained oblivious to the child's distress.

The audience by now was screaming at Stephen to turn around. When he eventually looked behind him and realised the enormity of his crime, he acted without hesitation. Leaping into the orchestra pit, he impaled himself on the conductor's baton.

It was the honourable thing to do.

I was watching the French television version of *You've Been Framed*, in which someone had sent in a video of a concert at which the lead singer of a band had 'crowd surfed' into the audience. Leaping theatrically back onto the stage, he tripped on a cable, lost his balance, and flailed comically towards the back of the stage before crashing head-first through the fabric of a giant speaker.

The Gods of rock'n'roll can be very cruel.

Stitch that, Kevin

Hollywood film star Kevin Bacon is perfectly at home on the film set, but slightly less so, it seems, on the rock stage, where he plies his secondary trade as the leader of the band The Bacon Brothers.

Their performance at the national convention of the US Democrat Party went down a storm. Buoyed by the audience response, Kevin decided to whip his guitar into the air to salute the crowd, in the process of which he delivered himself a severe blow to the head.

Afterwards nursing a sore head and a bruised ego, Kevin described it as one of those embarrassing 'maybe you're not a rock star' moments.

He must have felt like hiding his head in one of the speakers. Celebrity chef Jamie Oliver has also suffered from loss of motor skills.

Off yer bike

In May 2003, Jamie Oliver was booked to appear on *The Oprah Winfrey Show* in America. The programme's producers thought it would be a great idea for him to arrive on set on his trademark scooter.

'The floor was really polished and the tyres were brand new', Oliver later recalled. 'Before I knew it, I stacked it, flew about a metre in the air, and landed on my chest. I had a really silky body warmer on and I slid about three and a half metres with my arms in some sort of Superman pose, using my chin as a brake.'

The audience applauded wildly, under the impression that the whole performance had been planned. Jamie did not disabuse them.

Should the Naked Chef be allowed to get away so easily with naming his children Poppy Honey and Daisy Boo?

Conductor Sir Georg Solti found embarrassment in three-four time.

Blood in the orchestra pit

In 1976 Sir Georg Solti was in the middle of conducting a performance of Mozart's *The Marriage of Figaro* in Washington when he somehow contrived to stab himself in the forehead with his baton. Blood spurted profusely, but he staunched the flow with his handkerchief while bravely continuing to conduct the orchestra. Sir Georg managed to keep going until the opera reached a part where the singers are accompanied by a solo harpsichord, before rushing from the pit to receive first aid.

What a performance

Michael Caine began his theatrical career as a stage manager and occasional actor with the Horsham Repertory Company. His professional debut was an unmitigated disaster. The man who would become a double Oscar-winning actor walked onstage with his flies open, and forgot his only line.

Caine clearly rose above his adversity, but bad early experiences can stop careers in their tracks. Timothy Charles

Robert Noel Bentinck is the 12th Earl of Portland and, I'm sure you know, the man who voiced the 'Mind the gap' warning on the Piccadilly Line of the London Underground. As an actor he has had a long and successful career on stage and screen, but is probably best known for his role as David in the long-running BBC radio soap, *The Archers*. He also lays claim to being a computer programmer, website designer, author and house renovator. Unfortunately the career he most desired eluded him.

Disco killed the radio star

Actor Tim Bentinck has spent most of his adult life writing songs. His style, he says, is a cross between Jake Thackray and Ian Dury. But his hopes of forging a career as a singer-songwriter were dashed by cruel embarrassment.

He was in his late 20s before he was finally asked to perform his songs on stage. His brother-in-law booked him to perform at a Social Democrat Party fundraising dinner. A disco was booked to come on after his set.

Tim started playing, but was very conscious that his audience was much more interested in eating and talking. He ploughed on regardless, briefly managing to command the attention of the dinner guests when he accidentally knocked the music off the stand. 'At least that got a laugh', he says.

The chatter and laughter grew in volume as Tim soldiered on. 'No one was paying me any attention now', says Tim. 'Then halfway through what I thought was my best piece, the disco started with 'Jumping Jack Flash' and everyone got up to dance. I stopped, packed up my things and left by the back exit.'

Tim went on to star in a West End musical, perform in cabaret and panto, and even sing a duet in Disney's *101 Dalmatians, Part 2*, but never again performed his own songs in public.

Barbra Streisand was already an international superstar when embarrassment nearly ended her live performing career for good.

The way she was

Barbra Streisand had always been shy, but fought against the instinct to forge a hugely successful career as a singer and actor. Her live concerts were legendary. Then during a concert in Central Park in New York in 1967, she forgot the words to several songs. She was so mortified by the experience that she didn't perform in public again for 27 years.

Streisand is one of a great many successful performers who have suffered from stage fright. Lord Olivier was another. American pop star Donny Osmond had a panic attack during a performance in 1994 and thought he was going to black out. He developed an overwhelming fear of performing in public, of even being seen on the street, and recovered only after a long course of 'cognitive behavioural therapy'. Middle-of-the-road music lovers around the world can thank the science of psychology for giving Donny back to them.

Some people are more able than others to rise above embarrassment, though you might take the view that former Labour Home Secretary David Blunkett would have spared himself a lot of grief if an early public-speaking experience had discouraged him from a career in public life.

Not the real thing

As a teenager, David Blunkett, who'd been blind from birth, was asked to say a word of thanks at the end of a youth-club function.

'I reached out for what I presumed was the microphone', he recalls. 'Picking up the shapely object unfamiliar to one from the sheltered existence of the School for the Blind, I raised it to my lips and addressed the audience. It didn't seem to work. The truth then dawned – I was addressing the assembled throng, not through the microphone, but through a Coca-Cola bottle.'

Stage fright is more correctly known as 'performance anxiety', and strikes not just singers and actors, but anyone who steps in front of any kind of audience. Being asked to 'say a few words' in a business meeting or make a speech as best man at a wedding can present a terrifying prospect. Public speakers are the most common victims of this condition.

Like Donny Osmond, Barbra Streisand eventually learned to cope with her performance anxiety and returned to the stage. For others, fear of embarrassment is so severe that they hardly ever show their faces in public, convinced that they'll be mercilessly scrutinised and found wanting. Performance anxiety, unfortunately, doesn't seem to affect the critics.

The critics

The English writer Charles Lamb enjoyed great acclaim for his essays and poetry. But in 1807 his farce *Mr H*, performed at London's Drury Lane theatre, was a total disaster. The audience hated it and hissed their disapproval. Lamb, who was watching from the pit, was mortified, but joined in the hissing, explaining afterwards that he was 'damnably afraid of being taken for the author'.

Later he wrote angrily to a friend of his treatment by the critics among the Drury Lane audience.

> Mercy on us, that God should give his favourite children, men, mouths to speak with, to discourse rationally, to promise smoothly, to flatter agreeably, to encourage warmly, to counsel wisely, to sing with, to drink with, and to kiss with, and that they should turn them into mouths of adders ... and emit breath through them like distillations of aspic poison, to asperse and vilify the innocent labours of their fellow-creatures who are desirous to please them!
>
> Heaven be pleased to make the teeth rot out of them all, therefore!

Indignation is a classic response to embarrassment, the alternative being to dismiss such poisoned words as beneath contempt and unworthy of a response. It's not recorded how, or indeed if, the victims of the following barbs responded to their critics.

> 'Me no Leica.'
> > Dorothy Parker's entire review of the film of
> > Christopher Isherwood's *I Am a Camera*

> 'This is not a novel that should be tossed aside lightly. It should be thrown with great force.'
> > Dorothy Parker on Benito Mussolini's
> > *Claudia Particella*

'It's just so catastrophic I expected the audience to adopt the "brace" position in the stalls, as if on a crashing plane.'

Guardian film critic Peter Bradshaw on *Gigli*, starring Jennifer Lopez and Ben Affleck

'If white bread could sing it would sound like Olivia Newton John.'

Anon

The American novelist and book reviewer, Lev Grossman, has had his own reviews reviewed. Grossman wrote in *Time* magazine about how he had become the victim of an internet blogger calling himself Edward Champion, who had taken it upon himself to regularly attack him. His reviews had been derided and he had been personally dismissed as 'a chicken-head', 'preposterous', and 'irrelevant'. 'The first time I noticed Ed criticizing my writing, I e-mailed a response', says Grossman. 'His answer was so sarcastic it practically damaged my retinas.'

Which is why the usual advice is never respond to a critic. It only encourages them.

Many writers and performers maintain that they are indifferent to the opinions of critics, or claim they never even read their reviews. Most of them are lying.

Actress Helena Bonham Carter insists she's proud of the fact that her flamboyant dress style often finds her at the top of national newspaper 'worst dressed' lists, and was once voted the worst dressed actress at the Oscar ceremony. First prize for non-embarrassability, though, goes to US actress Halle Berry. Having survived the ridicule which greeted her hysterical Oscar acceptance speech for *Monster Ball*, she went on to commit the huge (creative if not financial) mistake of appearing in the film *Catwoman*. Of it, Connie Ogle in the *Miami Herald* wrote: '*Catwoman* doesn't belong on the big screen. It belongs in the litter box or to be scraped off the bottom of our shoes as we head quickly for another theater.'

Catwoman was nominated as Worst Film, and Halle Berry as Worst Actress, in the annual Golden Raspberry Awards or Razzies, presented as a sort of antidote to the excesses of the Oscars. The Razzies ceremony isn't usually graced by its winners, but extraordinarily, Berry actually turned up to collect her award and thanked the makers of *Catwoman* for 'putting me in a God-awful movie'. Now was that courage, or just an inspired piece of damage limitation? Let's be charitable and call it a bit of both.

Critics can get things embarrassingly wrong themselves, of course. The so-called experts responsible for these following criticisms (misguided or malicious) should, perhaps, have been required to fall upon their pens.

John Keats, who had been an apprentice to an apothecary, was once advised by a critic to go 'back to plasters, pills and ointment boxes'. Lord Byron called him 'a tadpole of the Lakes', and said his writing was 'a sort of mental masturbation … a bedlam vision produced by raw pork and opium'. Keats was so badly received as a poet during his lifetime, he asked for his gravestone to be inscribed: 'Here Lies One Whose Name Was Writ in Water.'

Herman Melville's *Moby Dick* was reviewed by *New Monthly Magazine* as 'maniacal … gibberish, screaming, like an incurable Bedlamite reckless of keeper or straight-jacket'.

William Wordsworth saw his poems dismissed as 'silly, infantile, nauseating and disgusting'.

And James Lorimer in the *British Review* wrote of Emily Brontë's *Wuthering Heights*: 'All the faults of *Jane Eyre* are magnified a thousandfold, and the only consolation which we have in reflecting upon it is that it will never be generally read.'

Gotcha

If you achieve success in the entertainment business and survive the critics, there are still your colleagues to watch out for. This is a dog-eat-dog world.

TV presenters like Ant and Dec, Jeremy Beadle and Noel Edmonds have built careers upon humiliating their fellow entertainers, targeting them in elaborate pranks designed to make them look as foolish as possible. Noel Edmonds' 'Gotcha Oscars' – awarded to more than 100 suckered celebrities – became so high-profile that the American Academy took legal action to make them drop the word Oscar.

One of the most famous Gotchas involved the BBC Radio 1 DJ Dave Lee Travis, whose Saturday morning show was infiltrated and sabotaged by a disguised Noel Edmonds and his team. When the scam was revealed, DLT went apoplectic with rage, famously shouting: 'You're a dead man, Edmonds.'

More recently, Michelin-starred chef Gordon Ramsay invited the Peter Pan of Pop, Cliff Richard, on to his television show *The F-Word*, as the latest celebrity to launch his own wine label. Cunningly, he manoeuvred Sir Cliff into a wine-tasting challenge, during which the singer was served wine from his own Portuguese vineyard. 'That's rubbish', pronounced Sir Cliff. 'I wouldn't pay for that. It's tainted. It tastes like vinaigrette.' Ramsay later claimed in a newspaper article that, after he told Sir Cliff he was drinking his own wine, he was told, sadly off camera, in no uncertain terms to 'fuck off'.

Cliff later told journalists that this accusation upset him so much he didn't sleep for four nights. He didn't seem unduly embarrassed about rubbishing his own wine, however. Perhaps Sir Cliff should thank himself lucky he didn't fall victim to Chris Morris.

No fool like a celebrity fool

In 2001 the comedy writer and performer Chris Morris produced a 'paedophile special' edition of his satirical television show *Brass Eye*.

According to its producers, the programme was designed as a response to the 'moral panic' prevalent in certain parts of the media, which had, among other things, prompted one man to launch a vicious assault on a paediatrician, mistaking her for a paedophile.

Various celebrities and other public figures were invited to take part in promoting a paedophile aware-ness campaign. They were then asked to read scripts containing a wide range of ludicrous assertions.

The Capital Radio DJ Neil Fox, for example, informed viewers that 'paedophiles have more genes in common with crabs than they do with you and me'. He added: 'Now that is scientific fact – there's no real evidence for it – but it *is* scientific fact.' MP Syd Rapson informed viewers that paedophiles were using 'an area of internet the size of Ireland', and comedian Richard Blackwood asserted that paedophiles can make com-puter keyboards emit noxious fumes in order to subdue children. Blackwood is seen sniffing a keyboard, and claims to be able to smell the fumes, which he says make him feel 'suggestible'.

And later made him feel acutely embarrassed, one would hope.

Television has so many ways to embarrass those who fall within its compass. Satirical shows from *That Was The Week That Was* to *Spitting Image* have ridiculed and humiliated generations of politicians and celebrities. Reality TV gives the celebrated and the uncelebrated an equal opportunity to self-harm. For those who are a little more circumspect, Chris Morris and Ant and Dec, or Sacha Baron Cohen (in the guise of Ali G or Borat), or perhaps Michael Moore or Louis Theroux will come and get you.

Some celebrities don't need any help; they are naturally embarrassing. Who can forget David Hasselhoff, of *Baywatch* fame, wearing a jacket adorned with flashing light bulbs, singing about freedom to young Germans tearing down the Berlin Wall? Or the profusely sweating Peter Andre at his grossly OTT wedding to model Jordan?

Few can escape the unblinking eye of the television camera.

Perfectly cooked egg on her face

Egg-boiling expert Delia Smith, in her capacity as director of her beloved Norwich City Football Club, was upset about the lack of vocal support that fans had been giving the team. Two-nil down to Manchester City, she snatched the microphone at half-time and harangued the crowd. Sounding as if she'd had a little too much of her own sherry trifle, she repeatedly bellowed: 'Where are you. Let's be having you.'

In an internet vote, 65 per cent of those who responded thought her performance had been 'excruciating'. A further 27 per cent were more generous and found it simply 'funny'.

Most Eurovision Song Contest entrants are firmly in the 'excruciating' category.

Nil points?

The year that Brotherhood of Man won the Eurovision Song Contest with 'Save Your Kisses For Me' was more memorable for the Finnish entry. The ditty was called 'Pump Pump' and sung by the rather rotund Fredi and his excitable bunch of Friends. The lyrics include 'let your hips go hippetty pump pump'. It made Lulu's 'Boom-Bang-A-Bang' seem positively profound.

For me, one of the most embarrassing moments on television, outside of the fictional antics of Ricky Gervais' David Brent or Larry David in *Curb Your Enthusiasm*, came on *Have I Got News For You*. Shortly after newspaper revelations about his 'cocaine-fuelled three-in-a-bed nights with prostitutes', the programme's host Angus Deayton had to endure a barrage of ridicule from regular team captains Paul Merton and Ian Hislop. The pair turned the entire programme into a remorseless and rather vicious onslaught on the hapless Deayton, who visibly struggled to keep smiling, and shortly afterwards was axed from the show.

And then there was that moment with the St John's ambulancemen.

To the rescue

The popular 1980s series *Kick Start* featured schoolchildren competing on motorbikes over a series of obstacles. In one famous incident, a young competitor, trying to negotiate a thin plank bridge, topples, along with his bike, into a fairly deep ditch.

An elderly, trench-coated St John's ambulanceman, toddling to the rescue, slips and rolls comically down into the ditch, followed almost immediately by an equally doddery colleague. The two men are clearly disorientated. The young motorcyclist, if I remember correctly, disdainfully climbs out of the ditch under his own steam, while his would-be rescuers roll about helplessly.

Michael Jackson qualifies for this book a hundred times over, but this performance was among his most embarrassing.

Embarrassment of the Millennium

At the 2002 MTV music awards, Britney Spears asked Michael Jackson to come on stage to receive a birthday cake, referring to him rather grandiosely as her personal 'artist of the millennium'. But the molten-faced singer gets completely the wrong end of the stick. Appearing on stage, and totally ignoring the impressive cake, he marches to the microphone and announces: 'Never did I imagine when I started out in the music business that I would one day be voted the *Artist of the Millennium*.'

The celebrity audience watches in stunned and mortified silence.

The road to self-destruction

There's an interesting theory going around (which I'm just making up) that everyone is born with the same amount of luck and it's just a matter of time before all the good and bad stuff in your life evens out. OK, not very likely, but it would explain why those who achieve fame and fortune seem to have to pay for it in other ways.

Take writers, for example. Once they've made a bit of a name for themselves, and their books start selling, publishers shove them out onto the publicity trail. It can be a perilous path.

The book what I didn't write

The Scottish writer Andrew O'Hagan was once interviewed at length on live TV in Chicago about a book he hadn't written. Too embarrassed to inform the presenter of his mistake, O'Hagan simply replied to questions as best he could and finally, after a tricky fifteen minutes or so, managed to take his leave with no one the wiser.

Deconstructive criticism

Poet Glyn Maxwell was invited to do a reading for some schoolchildren. Asked by one child what a particular poem, 'Seventh Day', was about, he explained in some detail what he had been trying to convey. When he'd finished, the child paused, looked him straight in the eye, and said: 'Why didn't you just write that then?'

All by myself

Booker Prize-winning author John Banville was roped in for a last-minute book-signing engagement in Miami. He sat there at a desk, with a pile of his books beside him and no punters in view. Eventually a woman approached him. He raised his pen expectantly, only to be told: 'I'm not going to buy your book, but you looked so lonely there, I thought I'd come and talk to you.'

More like a whimper

Had no one attended Michael Holroyd's first book

signing, it would have been fractionally better than what actually happened. The unhappy event took place at the Bedford Square Book Bang. Holroyd was positioned beside a wheelbarrow of his books, waiting for people to buy them and have them autographed. Nobody showed the remotest interest until finally a man strode up to him carrying a copy of his book, purchased on an earlier occasion, and announced that he wanted his money back, as it was 'not worth the paper it was written on'.

Holroyd said later that he felt he should qualify for the Guinness Book of Records as the first author to sell minus one copies of a book.

Noises off

David Harsent leads a double life as poet and crime-fiction writer. It was in his capacity as poet that he was invited along with three other writers to a bookshop reading. He arrived drunk, and proceeding to fall asleep on stage, snored through his colleagues' attempts to perform. He then woke, rushed to the toilet and vomited loudly (a ten-gallon tsunami, he reports), copiously and within full hearing range of the entire audience.

Some writers already have a high profile in other fields, but it doesn't afford them any protection.

Red but not read

Barry Humphries, in the guise of Australia's original desperate housewife, was hosting a late-night entertainment show, *An Audience with Dame Edna*, when he spotted Melvyn Bragg amid the celebrity audience.

'Ooooooh … I spy little Melvyn Bragg', shrieks Dame Edna. 'Melvyn is a famous novelist. How many novels have you written, Melvyn?' Bragg replies nervously that he thinks he has written about a dozen.

After a brief pause, Dame Edna adds with machine-gun delivery: '*Hands-up-everyone-who's-read-one-of-Melvyn's-books.*'

About three people put up their hands. 'You're going too fast, Melvyn', says Dame Edna. 'We can't keep up with you.'

And what about actors then? If you prick them, do they not bleed?

Win Tony Curtis for a weekend

Tony Curtis once volunteered to participate in a 'Win Tony Curtis for a Weekend' contest. 'They gave me away as a prize', he recalled. 'The woman who won was disappointed. She'd hoped for second prize … a new stove.'

Testing testing

In the broadcasting world, it's embarrassingly common for microphones to be switched on before brains are fully engaged. We'll look at some of the jewels in the crown of verbal gaffes in a minute, but first we reflect on the microphone's ability to embarrass people by pretending to be off when it is, in fact, decidedly on.

2006 was a vintage year.

In the bathroom

In August 2006, CNN news anchor Kyra Phillips was totally unaware that her microphone was still live when she took a 'bathroom break' during the broadcast of a speech by George Bush. Viewers watching the President could clearly hear Phillips talking about how her husband was 'handsome', 'genuinely loving' and 'a really passionate, compassionate, great, great human being'. Her sister-in-law did less well in the impromptu broadcast, dismissed as 'just a control freak'.

Politicians seem to be especially prone to stumbling into this particular embarrassment snare.

At the G8 summit in St Petersburg in July 2006, Tony Blair and George Bush inadvertently revealed a little more than they intended to, as they conducted their famous 'Yo Blair' conversation within range of a live microphone. George Bush revealed his subtle command of Middle Eastern politics with the following insightful analysis: 'You see, the thing is, what they need to do is to get Syria to get Hezbollah to stop doing this shit and it's over.'

And that was in response to Tony Blair's suggestion that he might go to the Middle East ahead of US Secretary of State, Condoleezza Rice. 'Because obviously if she goes out, she's got to succeed, as it were, whereas I can go out and just talk.' Which was Blair admitting that no one would expect him to achieve anything.

A minute is a long time in politics when you don't know you're being recorded. In July 1993, British Prime Minister John Major, believing that ITN cameras and microphones had been switched off, let slip the fact that he considered three members of his rebellious Cabinet (almost certainly Michael Howard, Peter Lilley and Michael Portillo) to be 'bastards'.

Major's gaffe revealed his true feelings, but former US President Ronald Reagan was, we must assume, joking when, while waiting to begin a radio address to the nation, he unintentionally told millions of listeners: 'I'm pleased to tell you that I just signed legislation which outlaws Russia forever. The bombing starts in five minutes.'

And it's not just politicians who fall into this particular trap. Former football player and manager Ron Atkinson put his lucrative TV commentary career into reverse in April 2004 when he said of Chelsea defender Marcel Desailly, after the team's defeat, and believing the microphone had been switched off: 'He's what's known in some schools as a fucking lazy thick nigger.' Atkinson denied having a racist bone in his body, but was nevertheless forced to resign his position at ITV and also lost his regular column in the *Guardian*.

In August 2006, Dean Jones, the former Australian Test batsman turned TV commentator, met a similar fate. He was sacked by his employers, Ten Sports, after being heard calling South African cricketer Hashim Amla a 'terrorist' on live television. During the fourth day's play between Sri Lanka and South Africa at Colombo, Amla, who is a devout Muslim, took the catch to dismiss Kumar Sangakkara. Jones was heard to say: 'The terrorist has got another wicket.'

Like Atkinson, Jones claimed that he thought the microphone was off, and despite fulsome apologies, was sacked.

Slips of the tongue

Sigmund Freud had a theory or two about verbal slips. He of course believed that they were not merely embarrassing, but also a signal of our innermost desires.

An open and shut case

In the late 19th century, the president of the lower house of Austria's parliament opened one particular session by announcing: 'I declare this meeting closed.'

This incident appears in Freud's *The Psychopathology of Everyday Life*. The psychoanalyst was certain that the error revealed the politician's real feelings, noting: 'The president secretly wished he was already in a position to close the sitting, from which little good was to be expected.'

Just the other day, my hairdresser, Rose, was talking to me about tattoos while blow-drying my barnet. Her flamboyantly gay colleague, Peter, contributed the fact that he had a rather nice tattoo. 'Oh yes', said Rose. 'It's a big fairy.' There was a distinctly frosty pause, after which Peter put her straight: 'It's an *angel*', he said. You could have cut the atmosphere with a pair of styling scissors.

Examine the following verbal gaffes as closely as you like; I suspect you'll struggle to find any deep meaning behind them. They do certainly reflect how difficult it is to keep the rich and complex English language under control, and just maybe there's the odd Freudian slip in there somewhere.

The verbal gaffe is a speciality of the sports commentator.

'We welcome World Service listeners to the Oval, where the bowler's holding the batsman's willy.'

It was an unedifying image. The great radio broadcaster and cricket commentator Brian Johnston had intended to inform listeners to Radio 4's *Test Match Special* coverage of the 1976 match between England and the West Indies: 'The bowler's Holding. The batsman's Willey.' He was referring to the West Indies bowler Michael Holding and the English batsman Peter Willey.

This is a classic, though some spoilsports contend apocryphal, example of the sporting commentator's fine tradition of verbal faux pas. Unchallenged stars of the genre, however, are David Coleman and the inimitable Murray Walker.

Sports presenter David Coleman delighted us with pearls of wisdom such as:

> 'And here's Moses Kiptanui, the nineteen-year-old Kenyan, who turned twenty a few weeks ago.'

> 'Don't tell those coming in the result of that fantastic match, but let's have another look at Italy's winning goal ...'

But retired Grand Prix racing commentator Murray Walker is the undisputed champion of this fine art. His endearing gaffes helped turn him into an official national treasure. His fan club has produced Murray Walker T-shirts bearing the logo 'Unless I'm very much mistaken ... I'm very much mistaken', though no one has ever been able to prove that he ever actually said it. But he was definitely responsible for these following gems, plucked from his expansive back catalogue.

> 'I imagine that the conditions in those cars are totally unimaginable.'

> 'And here comes Damon Hill in the Williams. This car is absolutely unique – except for the one following it, which is identical.'

> 'Do my eyes deceive me, or is Senna's Lotus sounding a bit rough?'

'There is nothing wrong with the car except that it is on fire.'

'René Arnoux is coming into the pits ... let's stop the startwatch.'

Murray Walker refuses to admit that he has ever been embarrassed by his slips of the tongue. 'I get very excited', he explains, 'and sometimes the words come out in the wrong order. We all make mistakes in life. We are all human beings. I am a human being, I make mistakes.'

Sports commentators and pundits on the other side of the Atlantic are equally prone to getting their message in a muddle.

'It is beyond my apprehension.'
Danny Ozark, baseball team manager,
Philadelphia Phillies

'Well, that was a cliff-dweller.'
New York Mets manager Wes Westrum,
about a close baseball game

'If there's a pile-up they'll have to give some of the players artificial insemination.'
Curt Gowdy, TV network announcer, commenting
on an American football game played on a
waterlogged field

'One of the reasons Arnold Palmer is playing so well is that, before each tee shot, his wife takes out his balls and kisses them ... Oh my god! What have I just said?'
Unidentified US commentator

That last contributor sounds as if he might have been sufficiently mortified to hurl himself from his lofty commentary box. It's a privilege, but not always a blessing, to have the opportunity to speak to the nation, as many politicians will confirm, Deputy Prime Minister John Prescott prominent among them: 'The Green Belt was a Labour achievement ... and we are going to build on it.' This from the man who after a long and arduous flight once remarked: 'It's great to be back on terracotta.'

That's close enough for me. And then there was Tory Prime Minister, John Major: 'When your back's against the wall it's time to turn round and fight.'

But we must cross the Atlantic and peer into the White House to observe the master at work. George W. Bush employs an army of advisers and scriptwriters to ensure that his official speeches are gaffe-free. What must they think when they observe his attempts to fly solo, nosediving into the ground at every opportunity? Let's start by looking at George on the subject of child literacy.

'Rarely is the question asked: "Is our children learning?"'

'You teach a child to read and he or her will be able to pass a literacy test.'

'The illiteracy level of our children are appalling.'

It would be nice to think that these following linguistic foul-ups don't actually reflect what he was really trying to say.

'I was not pleased that Hamas has refused to announce its desire to destroy Israel.'

4 May 2006

'It's in our country's interests to find those who would
do harm to us and get them out of harm's way.'

28 April 2005

These remaining examples are just plain daft.

'Free societies will be allies against these hateful few
who have no conscience, who kill at the whim of a hat.'

17 September 2004

'I am mindful not only of preserving executive powers
for myself, but for predecessors as well.'

29 January 2001

'The senator ... can't have it both ways. He can't take
the high horse and then claim the low road.'

17 February 2000

'They misunderestimated me.'

6 November 2000

And you can't blame them.

* * *

I'll leave you with my favourite verbal gaffe of all time. Not
from the mouth of a politician, nor a sports commentator or
newsreader, but from one of the original celebrity chefs –
Johnny Craddock. After he and his wife had served up a
masterclass on the culinary possibilities of combining flour,
milk and eggs, he delivered the immortal line: 'I hope all your
doughnuts turn out like Fanny's.'

CHAPTER EIGHT

EMBARRASSMENT AT PLAY

Sport provides us with a perfect arena in which to fail spectacularly. Designed as it is to test our physical skills, it will also, therefore, remorselessly expose our limitations. And, as in so many areas of life, the bigger we are, the harder we fall.

As amateur sportsmen and women we can only dabble at the edges of sporting embarrassment. The professionals go in for this sort of thing on a much grander scale, often in front of thousands, and sometimes, via television, millions of onlookers.

But calamitous misadventures occur regularly wherever sporting horns are locked. They happen to the biggest stars of sport, and they happen to you and me. Well, they certainly happen to me.

Sporting embarrassment can be merciless, striking often at the very moment of glittering achievement, as was the experience of one of Britain's top international hurdlers.

A hurdle too far

Alan Pascoe was blessed with natural athleticism – a perfect combination of physical coordination and spatial awareness, which took him to gold in the technically demanding 400m hurdles at the 1974 Commonwealth Games in Christchurch, New Zealand. But where were those skills just minutes later?

As he completed his lap of honour, still a little drunk on adrenalin perhaps, he couldn't resist treating the cheering crowd to one last demonstration of his talent for effortlessly clearing the three-foot-high hurdle. It was a mistake.

Looking more like a newborn foal than an international athlete, he clattered into the hurdle, collapsed across it, and fell heavily to the ground. The crowd roared with laughter. Unfortunately this simply encouraged the clearly embarrassed Pascoe to try again. Another ungainly clash with the hurdle sent Pascoe tumbling earthwards a second time. Sensing that a third failure might cause spectators serious damage from laughing too much, Pascoe again approached the hurdle, but this time pushed it to the ground – removing the temptation to embarrass himself further.

But the damage was done. Lest he forget the experience, the British Sports Photographers Association thoughtfully presented him with a framed shot of the incident. Significantly, Pascoe didn't allow his embarrassment to distract him, going on to win that year's European title. Later he would become a multimillionaire businessman. None of which, of course, detracts from his most memorable achievement – as the man who fell on his arse celebrating victory.

Embarrassing lapses in skill or concentration can have far-reaching consequences. They can end careers, or in one thankfully isolated case, result in death. During the 1994 World Cup, the Colombian footballer Andres Escobar scored an own goal in a match against the United States, turning a harmless-looking cross past his own goalkeeper to give the opposition an unexpected 2-1 victory. He wasn't the first footballer to make such an embarrassing mistake, but the first, I think, to pay for it with his life. On his return to Colombia he was shot dead by someone who had lost money betting on the game.

More usually, embarrassment falls short of being fatal, though death can sometimes seem preferable at the time.

One shoe on and one shoe off

During the 1953 Masters golf tournament at Augusta, Georgia, British amateur golfer John de Forest, playing the 13th hole, hit a shot into a shallow brook, just a couple of feet from the bank. The safe option was to take a one-shot penalty and drop the ball on dry land before attempting to make further progress. But de Forest decided to go for the much more difficult option of trying to hit the ball from where it lay in several inches of water. All eyes were on him as he prepared to make this extremely adventurous shot. De Forest took off his right shoe, then his right sock. He then rolled up his right trouser leg to just above the knee. He stood back from the bank and practised his swing. Then, approaching the ball, and temporarily taking leave of his senses, he planted his bare right foot firmly on the bank, and his left foot (still in his shoe) in the water. Those there that day say he was almost weeping with embarrassment as he awkwardly hacked the ball onto dry land.

It's the sort of thing I can imagine doing myself. I've certainly done some amazingly embarrassing things on a golf course, and still judge the success of a round of golf by how few balls I lose in the deep rough or hook out of bounds. But my most mortifying sporting experience was on a football pitch. I've been searching for a photograph of the event. Taken by my wife (thank you very much, Di), it captures a moment that, though it happened many years ago, is as painfully vivid in my memory as if it were yesterday.

I have really only ever had one sporting hero – the Tottenham Hotspur and England football genius Jimmy Greaves. His extraordinary goalscoring skills were enough to make me forgive his general reluctance to tackle anyone, his alcoholism and, towards the end of his career, a rather unfortunate perm. I idolised him.

So it was literally a dream come true when, in the early 1980s, I got the opportunity to play against him in a charity match in Birmingham. I was an enthusiastic player, but not over-endowed with natural talent. My usual role was to run around a lot and distract the opposition. But on this occasion I wanted to do more than that. I wanted to dazzle.

By midway through the second half I had perhaps touched the ball a couple of times, and done nothing to impress the quite sizeable crowd, or my hero. Suddenly a defence-splitting pass put me through clear on goal, with only the keeper to beat …

And then the referee blew his whistle. Offside!

'Offside?' I shouted. 'You must be joking, referee. I was never offside.'

Which was when Jimmy Greaves spoke to me. Or rather he shouted at me: 'Don't fucking argue with the referee, you wanker', or something to that effect. Then he turned and walked out of my life forever.

I've now found the photograph. It doesn't, as I'd thought, actually capture Jimmy's admonishing finger – just the moment when the referee signalled I was offside, and triggered my humiliation.

* * *

Embarrassment can be particularly severe on those sports-people guilty of celebrating their achievements prematurely.

Not driving but waving

With a comfortable lead on the final lap of the 1991 Canadian Grand Prix, British racing driver Nigel Mansell decided it was high time to celebrate. The future world champion slowed his Williams car dramatically and began to drive one-handed while waving to the Montreal crowd. With less than half a mile to go he slowed even further, then mysteriously stopped completely, allowing Brazilian driver Nelson Piquet through to win. 'I was winning and taking it easy', said Mansell, claiming that: 'The engine just stopped.' Embarrassment makes it difficult for us to acknowledge our mistakes. Formula One insiders maintain that Mansell accidentally flicked the 'kill' switch on his steering wheel (which shuts the engine down) while pulling an arm free to wave at the crowd.

Mansell was no stranger to public embarrassment, having painfully bumped his head on a beam while being lifted onto the podium after winning the Austrian Grand Prix in 1987. In a television interview later that afternoon, commentator Murray Walker famously asked Mansell where it hurt, as he simultaneously prodded the prominent bump on the racing driver's head.

Nigel Mansell wasn't the first person to suffer from premature celebration.

The last post

Way ahead of the field and with the winning post in

sight, jockey Bill Shoemaker, riding Gallant Man, stood up in the stirrups to salute the crowd at the 1957 Kentucky Derby. Unfortunately he had mistaken the half-furlong pole for the winning post. By the time he had realised his error it was too late. William Hartack on Iron Liege had swept past him to victory.

Give a little whistle

In the last minute of a football match against Blackpool at Highbury in 1955, fullback Dennis Evans, hearing the final whistle, kicked the ball into his own net in celebration. But the whistle had come from the crowd and referee Frank Coultas awarded the goal. It would have been even more embarrassing for Evans had Arsenal not been already 4-0 up.

He's behind you

British athletics hero Steve Ovett has always denied that there was any arrogance in his habit of waving to the crowd, and signalling 'I LOVE YOU' to his girlfriend, after taking the lead in the home stretch.

That may, or may not, be true, but his habit certainly tripped him up in a 5,000m event at Crystal Palace in 1980. Coming into the straight, he kicked past John Treacy of Ireland. The trademark wave was duly proffered and the crowd roared. But the spectators weren't cheering Ovett. They had seen what he hadn't – that Treacy had kicked again, dipping at the line, a fraction of an inch ahead of Ovett.

Kenyan marathon runner Robert Cheruiyot raised his hand to acknowledge the cheers of the crowd as he approached the tape in the 2006 Chicago Marathon, but then slipped, crashing onto his back just a yard from the finish. His momentum carried him over the line to victory, but the pain from a severe blow to the back of the head, and the bizarre manner of his win, somewhat took the edge off things.

Sporting celebrations, premature or otherwise, can often result in embarrassment.

Late faller

Young jockey Fergal Lynch was quickly brought down to earth after winning on Kris Kin at Chester in 2003. As he passed the winning post on the 20-1 shot in the Ormonde Stakes, Lynch stood up and waved his whip towards the crowd to celebrate the biggest win of his career. As he was doing so, his frisky mount veered suddenly to the right, throwing an embarrassed Lynch to the ground.

Hitting the wall

Argentinian football striker Martin Palermo was delighted when he scored in extra time for Villarreal against Levante in the 2001 Spanish Cup. Palermo rushed to the crowd to celebrate, jumping onto a small pitch-side wall which promptly collapsed. The Argentinian was carried off on a stretcher and taken to hospital with a broken ankle that kept him out of the game for months.

Footballers seem to make a habit of doing these sort of things. Arsenal captain Patrick Vieira once tore a hamstring while sliding to celebrate his goal against Manchester United. In 2003, Manchester City's Shaun Goater celebrated a team-mate's goal by kicking an advertising hoarding, injured his knee and had to be substituted. Five years earlier, Goater had fallen and broken his arm celebrating a goal in a crucial relegation match. Celestine Babayaro broke his leg while performing his trademark somersault celebrations on his Chelsea debut in a preseason friendly. But here's my favourite ...

Giving the crowd the finger

Paulo Diogo of Swiss League side Servette celebrated his goal against Schaffhausen by jumping into the crowd, catching his wedding ring on a fence and tearing off the top half of his finger. To add insult to, very painful, injury, he was booked by the referee, Florian Etter, for 'over-celebrating' his goal.

He managed to retrieve the severed digit, but unfortunately surgeons were unable to reattach it.

And injuries can even occur on the sidelines. Arsenal footballer Perry Groves was confined to the substitutes' bench during a match, but managed to knock himself out after hitting his head on the roof of the dugout as he leapt up to celebrate a goal.

In such cases I imagine the embarrassment didn't fully kick in until the worst of the pain had subsided. But there's a certain amount of assumption on my part here. Footballers in particular, but sportsmen and women in general, need a lot of self-belief, even arrogance, to excel. That arrogance, coupled to a refusal to admit mistakes, must protect them to some extent from the full impact of their embarrassing behaviour, or at least speed their recuperation.

Nick Faldo probably no longer agonises over his attempt to be sarcastic about the journalists who had been criticising him, by thanking them 'from the heart of my bottom', after his 1992 Open Victory at Muirfield. His attempt to sing 'My Way', however, should still cause him some shame.

Arsenal captain Tony Adams attracted considerable oppro-
brium for his alcoholism, nightclub fights and imprisonment
for drunk-driving, but embarrassment pursued him onto the
field as well. Playing away to Manchester United in 1989, the
defender sliced an attempted clearance past his own goalkeeper,
denying his team a victory in the title race. The next day he
was pictured as a donkey on the back page of a newspaper,
and a reputation was born. Adams had to bear the humiliation
of crowds chanting 'Donkey' at him for years. But there was
worse to come.

Break an arm

Tony Adams was over the moon when his teammate
Steve Morrow scored the goal which gave their side a
2-1 victory over Sheffield Wednesday to win the 1993
League Cup trophy. After the final whistle, amid the
team celebrations, Adams couldn't resist lifting Morrow
onto his shoulders. Unfortunately, no sooner was he
up, than he was down, landing awkwardly and breaking
his arm. As the other Arsenal players continued their
revelry, Adams was anxiously tending the injured
Morrow and calling for medical backup.

Morrow left the Wembley pitch on a stretcher with
an oxygen mask clamped to his face. Adams was so
upset that he had to be cajoled into climbing the steps
to receive the trophy on behalf of his victorious team.

For many, sporting embarrassment begins at school, during
the ritual humiliation of the selection of sides. Author Martin
Plimmer had been a big, strong, but uncoordinated schoolboy,
and was invariably 'last pick' for every team game. On the
cricket field, he was sent to the most distant boundary where
he was thought likely to do the least damage. He would stand

there, flapping away flies, contemplating an idyllic sport-free future – or as he puts it in his semi-autobiographical novel *King of the Castle*:

> Every week I stood on a horizon where no cricket ball had ever strayed, studying the grass around me. I became friends with worms. I watched worms grow up, raise families and die.

Suddenly, his reverie was disturbed by the sound of his name being shouted. 'Plimmer!' went the cry. 'Catch the ball.' Peering into the sky, Martin identified the object in question. Stretching out his arms in the general direction of the ball's trajectory, cupping his hands in the fashion he dimly recalled being instructed by the PE teacher, he took the only further precaution he could think of – he closed his eyes. If he couldn't see the ball, perhaps it wouldn't be there. This, as we have seen, is an instinctive human response to almost any embarrassing situation. But the ball, of course, didn't go away. It completed its inevitable course, passing effortlessly through Martin's prayerfully proffered hands, landing squarely on his unyielding forehead and causing him to crumple, semi-senseless, to the ground.

The pain was irrelevant; very real at the time, of course, but long since forgotten. Not so the associated derision dished out by his unsympathetic school chums. 'Plimmer', they observed, 'you're bloody useless'.

To this day, Martin hates all sport. He runs a mile (or rather doesn't) at even the mention of competitive activity. It brings back too many embarrassing memories. Much better not to take part.

But not taking part is not an option for the professional sportsperson.

By any normal standards, Tim Henman's tennis career has been an enormous success. He has remained in the top echelon of the game for more than a decade, though never, as the British press are keen to remind him, winning any of the four prestigious Open events, and more specifically, never winning Wimbledon. This, according to many observers, makes Henman a failure and a source of national embarrassment.

But what does Tiger Tim think? In the 2006 Wimbledon tournament, Henman 'crashed out' to world number one Roger Federer in straight sets, winning only a handful of games in the process. This, chorused the press, was an embarrassing defeat. Indeed, commentators during the game suggested that embarrassment caused by Federer's obvious superiority had contributed to Henman's poor performance.

In the after-match interviews, Henman was asked if he had wanted a hole to open up for him to crawl into. But Tiger Tim was singularly unabashed, insisting that there was no disgrace in being beaten by 'the best player I have ever competed against'. But is that what he really felt? Admitting to being embarrassed would be ... well ... embarrassing.

Some sportsmen, of course, are unable to conceal their embarrassment in defeat.

A knockout disguise

Floyd Patterson had been a great heavyweight boxing champion, the first man ever to regain the world title.

But when he came up against Sonny Liston in 1962 he was no longer at the peak of his powers, and Liston was looking unbeatable. Patterson's manager had been against the match, but his fighter, a quiet but fiercely proud man, wanted to test himself against the huge-punching Liston, so the fight was arranged.

With two left hooks and a right, Liston knocked out Patterson after two minutes and six seconds of the first round.

Patterson was so humiliated (and battered and bruised) that he left the Chicago venue wearing glasses, a false beard and moustache.

Being a soft Southerner, I've never had much time for Rugby League, despite a fondness for the eccentric 1960s commentator Eddie ('up and under') Waring. But one moment in this particular sport's history sticks vividly in my memory.

The last kick

The 1968 Rugby League Challenge Cup final was fought out between Leeds and Wakefield in front of 97,938 spectators. But the Wembley pitch was so water-logged that the players often looked like sixteen-stone unsynchronised swimmers.

Two minutes from the end, Leeds appeared to have an unassailable 11-7 lead, when Wakefield's Ken Hirst hacked the ball through the puddles and over the line for a try between the posts. The score was now 11-10, and the simple conversion would give Wakefield a dramatic last-minute victory.

A kick in front of the posts is a complete formality, particularly for such a seasoned goal-kicker as Wake-field's Don Fox, rated one of the best players of his day. He took a few steps back, then came forward and struck the ball, slicing it wide of the post. The Leeds players leapt with joy. Wakefield had lost. Fox fell flat on his face and later left the field in tears. He never played again.

Snatching defeat from the jaws of victory is never easy to bear.

Major bogey

It looked like French golfer Jean Van de Velde couldn't lose. Beginning the last hole in the last round of the 1999 British Open, he needed to complete it in six shots or less to take the title.

He drove his first shot, slicing it way to the right. His second shot hit a grandstand and bounced into deep rough. But he still had four shots in hand. His next shot landed in the water. He 'took a drop' which incurred a one-shot penalty. His next shot landed in a sand trap. His sixth stroke finally landed on the green, eight feet from the hole. He made the putt to finish on a disastrous triple-bogey seven. This put him into a three-way play-off with Justin Leonard of the USA and Britain's Paul Lawrie, which Lawrie eventually won.

Like Tim Henman, Van de Velde refused to concede to interviewers that his failure had been humiliating. 'No one died out there', he insisted. Mind you, some years later he did campaign to allow men to take part in women's competitions. 'I'll shave my legs and wear a kilt if I have to', he said. Now that would have been embarrassing.

Dressing up as a woman is one way to respond to embarrassment. Bullshitting is another.

Many a slip

During the 1972 Ashes Test match against Australia at Manchester's Old Trafford ground, England put in a particularly poor performance in the field, dropping a succession of easy catches. Fast-bowler John Snow was a particular culprit, failing to cling on to a couple of 'dollies'. His furious captain Ray Illingworth banished him to the far boundary to watch worms grow up and have children. Illingworth then proceeded to watch a ball drop through his own hands, bounce off his chest and plop gently to the ground.

Afterwards, the clearly embarrassed Yorkshireman went on television to say that Old Trafford was 'the worst ground in the country for sighting the ball'.

It's that round red thing, Ray, coming towards you.

* * *

At the 2004 Athens Olympics, Paula Radcliffe said she felt 'depressed, embarrassed and ashamed' after breaking down 6km from the end of the race. She tried to restart, before slumping by the side of the road in tears. The experience, she said, had been the most traumatic of her life. She was to shed more bodily fluids, though not tears this time, in the following year's London Marathon.

Call me old-fashioned, or sensitive, or odd, but I think going to the toilet is a private thing, best done out of the public gaze. Caught short on a long car journey, I will divert to the countryside and walk miles into the fields to avoid any possibility of being observed. Even there I worry that someone with a telescope could be watching from a distant hilltop, or Martians peering through whatever it is they use to keep an eye on us.

So what exactly went through Paula's mind when, at 22 miles into the London Marathon, she felt an overwhelming need to empty her bladder? Clearly less inhibited than me, she proceeded, in front of millions of television viewers, to crouch by the roadside to complete what she later described as 'an embarrassing necessity'. She did, of course, go on to win the event by a clear five minutes – enough time, I'd have thought, to have found some proper facilities. Afterwards, she said she wanted to 'apologise to the nation'. But what about the Martians?

Embarrassment in sport is more often the result of straight-forward blunders.

Back of the net

It's tough being a goalkeeper. Even small errors can look terrible, particularly if they result in letting in a goal. The otherwise illustrious career of Leeds and England keeper Gary Sprake was spoiled by one of the most embarrassing mistakes in the history of football.

It happened back in 1967 when Leeds were playing away at Liverpool. Sprake had the ball in his hands and had brought back his arm to throw the ball to one of his defenders, when he noticed the player was being closely marked. His attempt to prevent himself releasing the ball caused him to spin round and throw the ball into the back of his own net.

His abject embarrassment was latched onto by the home supporters, who greeted Sprake when he came out for the second half with a chorus of the big Des O'Connor hit of the time, 'Careless Hands'.

Poor Gary Sprake is certainly up there in the highest echelons of sporting blunderers, but he has company.

Out-gummed

Welterweight boxer Ralph Walton was knocked out in 10½ seconds in a bout at Lewiston, Maine, on 29 September 1946. After the bell sounded for the start of the contest, his opponent Aurele 'Al' Couture strode across the ring and struck him while he was still adjusting his gum shield in his corner. The 10½ seconds includes the 10 seconds needed to count him out.

Sometimes goalkeepers don't see it coming either.

Not a prayer

Senhor Isadore Irandir of the Brazilian team Rio Preto had to live with the ignominy of letting in the fastest goal to be scored in football history – after just three seconds.

From the kick-off in the game between Corinthians and Rio Preto at Bahia Stadium in 1974, the ball was passed to Roberto Rivelino, who scored with a left-foot drive from the halfway line. The ball went past the ear of Senhor Irandir while he was on his knees finishing prematch prayers in the goalmouth.

Embarrassing lapses in concentration, or failures of motor skills, can occur in any sport.

Splutterfly

In the 100m butterfly event at the 1960 Rome Olympics, American swimmer Carolyn Wood dived into the pool, swam one length, turned and disappeared below the surface of the water. For a few worrying moments it looked as if she had become the first swimmer to drown during the Olympic Games.

She eventually surfaced, spluttering and grasping the lane rope, as her coach dived fully clothed into the water to help. Carolyn later told reporters she had got a big mouthful of water and couldn't go on.

Miss Wood gained some relief from her embarrassment by winning a gold medal in the in 4x100m freestyle relay at the same Olympic Games.

Too embarrassed to ask for directions?

In the 1929 Rose Bowl, the big American college football game, the California Bears centre, Roy Riegels, committed what is widely considered the biggest blunder in the history of the US sport.

Picking up a loose ball during the game against Georgia Tech, Roy got bumped and spun round; finding himself in the clear, he sprinted towards the goal line 64 yards away. Unfortunately he was heading in the wrong direction.

He was chased by his own teammate, Benny Lom, who was screaming at him to stop, but couldn't make himself heard above the roar of the crowd. In the commentary box, the radio announcer Graham McNamee was shouting: 'Am I crazy? Am I crazy? Am I crazy?'

Lom eventually brought Riegels down with a flying tackle just a yard from his own line.

Riegels' extraordinary gaffe effectively cost the Bears the title. But it also won him a variety of sponsorship deals for upside-down cakes, clocks with hands which went backwards ... and the lifelong nickname 'Wrong Way Riegels'.

The hop, trip and throw

The big blond Finnish javelin thrower Seppo Henrik Räty was not a serious contender at the 1987 World Championships. As if to prove the fact, he made a horrific hash of his first throw.

At the end of his run he put in the customary hitch kick to get one leg behind the other as a fulcrum, but somehow got them in a knot, tripped and stuck his javelin into the ground two feet in front of him – and still behind the throwing line. He'd registered the first minus distance in the sport.

But Räty's embarrassment served only to inspire him. He picked himself up, dusted himself down, blushed sheepishly no doubt, then went on to become world champion with his final throw ... beating his nearest rival by a clear metre.

Sometimes sporting disaster is caused by factors outside the victim's control ... not that it necessarily makes it any easier to bear, or any less embarrassing.

Deflowered

The 1984 Olympic Modern Pentathlon competition was very closely contested. Towards the end of the final event, the 4,000m cross country, the favourite, Daniele Masala of Italy, was passed by Svante Rasmuson of Sweden. It looked as if the Swede only had to stay upright for the last 100m to win gold. Until 20m from the finishing line, Rasmuson rounded the last turn, skidded, recovered his balance, only to fall over a potted plant that the organisers had placed to decorate the course. Masala passed him to win the gold. Rasmuson never came so close to winning an Olympic title again.

Many sportsmen down the years have claimed that their failure was the result of faulty equipment: the wrong tip on a snooker cue, the wrong studs, or bat or ball – and perhaps even the wrong swimming trunks.

Not waving but ...

British swimmer Duncan Goodhew was taking part in a competition when the cord on his swimming trunks broke. 'It was terrible', he recalls. 'I was swimming backstroke.'

Most people will have little sympathy for sportsmen suffering the humiliation of being caught taking performance-enhancing drugs. Cycling, one of the most physically demanding of sports, has seen many of its top performers exposed as drug cheats, their reputations torn to shreds. Even the manner of their exposure can be embarrassing.

It's all gone pear-shaped

Riding in the 1978 Tour de France, Belgian cyclist Michael Pollentier conquered the murderous Alpe d'Huez to win the 16th stage of the race and take the Yellow Jersey.

He knew that, when he presented himself at the doping control, there was a strong likelihood that the officials would discover a large quantity of the illegal stimulant alupin sloshing around inside him.

Pollentier had therefore taken the precaution of equipping himself with a 'pear'. A rubber bulb was tucked into his armpit to squeeze drug-free urine down a tube which passed between his buttocks and emerged under his penis.

All would have been fine, except that the system developed a blockage and Pollentier struggled to produce a specimen. The doctor grew impatient and then suspicious (at Pollentier's exaggerated chicken-wing motions, presumably), and eventually pulled down the cyclist's shorts to expose his little pipe. Disqualification and bitter ignominy followed.

Sport cruelly exposes failure and error in referees, umpires and other officials as much as it does in players.

At the 2006 World Cup finals in Germany, top English football referee Graham Poll suffered the embarrassment of being sent home by FIFA after forgetting to send off a player after he had given him two yellow cards. Poll, who'd had a realistic chance of being chosen to referee the World Cup final, made his blunder while officiating the game between Australia and Croatia. He did eventually give the Croatian defender Josip Simunic his marching orders, but not until he had committed a third bookable offence.

It's certainly no easy job being a sports official. Referees, umpires and judges face persistent criticism that they are incompetent, corrupt, biased and myopic – or just failed athletes. We all make mistakes at work, but few of us have to put up with thousands of people screaming 'You're a bastard!' while giant screens replay our error and TV pundits dissect the decision with the aid of hi-tech graphics.

Not so Grand National

The 1993 Grand National was an event, in fact a non-event, which chief starter Keith Brown will never be allowed to forget.

At 3.58pm, Brown pulled the lever that should have hoisted the starting tape to allow the 39 runners and riders to set off around the hazardous Aintree course. In the high wind, the tape somehow managed to wrap itself around a number of the jockeys and their horses. Brown waved his red flag to stop the race, but not before six horses had reached the first fence.

At 4.03pm he tried again, with a similar result – nearly throttling a couple of jockeys. The red flag was waved again. This time, all but nine of the riders failed to see it and charged off down the course. Lack of communication between course officials led to eleven horses completing an entire circuit and seven horses running the whole 4.5-mile course before the whole sorry mess was declared null and void.

The unfortunate Keith Brown had to be given a police escort through the gauntlet of angry punters – his embarrassment temporarily deflected by fear.

You're colour blind, ref

Football referee Keith Butcher once awarded Everton a penalty when it should have been a free kick to West Bromwich Albion. Before another match, he didn't notice that both teams were wearing the same colour until a linesman pointed it out. He later admitted that he'd been unable to tell the difference between red and yellow cards. A fully qualified League referee, he was chronically colour-blind.

Everything stops for tea

Terrible timing by an unnamed official timekeeper was responsible for denying South African marathon runner Johannes Coleman an official world record. At the finish of the 1938 Natal Marathon, Coleman arrived at the Alexander Park Stadium in Pietermaritzburg with a huge lead over his nearest rival and more than three minutes inside the world record. Reaching the finishing tape, Coleman discovered to his dismay that the chief timekeeper had rather underestimated him, and was still in the tea room. Coleman never did set an official world record.

I hope Coleman was allowed a few minutes alone with the timekeeper, once he had got his breath back.

You cannot be awake

John McEnroe wouldn't have approved. During the 1964 first round Wimbledon tennis match between Clark Graebner of South Africa and Abe Segal of the United States, it suddenly became apparent to all involved that something was amiss with one of the line judges.

A ball had landed well beyond the baseline but had not been called out. Closer inspection revealed that the judge, a Mrs Dorothy Cavis-Brown, her arms folded, legs crossed, head on one side, was fast asleep.

Segal went over and tapped her on the shoulder to rouse her from her slumbers. Afterwards, Mrs Cavis-Brown insisted that she had only had a single gin at lunchtime, but she was never invited to officiate at Wimbledon again.

Embarrassment can lurk in a golf bag.

In July 2001, Ian Woosnam's Open chances were scuppered when he was docked two strokes for carrying fifteen instead of fourteen clubs. The mistake was made by his caddie Miles Byrne – but it was Woosnam who paid the price. Surprisingly perhaps, Woosnam didn't punch his caddie on the nose, nor did he sack him – until several weeks later when Byrne overslept and failed to turn up in time for the final day of the Scandinavian Masters tournament.

In sport, sometimes you just can't get the staff.

Losing his bottle

American soccer team trainer Jack Coll made a unique contribution to the inaugural World Cup competition in Uruguay in 1930.

It happened during the USA's semi-final against Argentina. The South American side had just scored a controversial goal. Shouting abuse at the referee as he went, Jack ran onto the pitch to attend to an injured player. Throwing down his medical bag, he broke a bottle of chloroform, inhaled the fumes and keeled over.

He had to be helped from the field by his players, to the great amusement of the 80,000 spectators.

Three wheels on my wagon

During the Portuguese Grand Prix in 1991, Nigel Mansell pulled off the course for a routine pit stop, including a tyre change. One of the mechanics, struggling to remove a cross-threaded wheel nut, raised his arm in a gesture which looked like he was saying he had finished his job. The man operating the jack lowered the car. Mansell drove on. As he came out of the pit, the back wheel came off. The crew chased up the pit lane and replaced the wheel, but Mansell was disqualified, effectively ending his chances of overtaking his main rival Ayrton Senna in the 1991 title race.

I wonder what that mechanic is doing now. Endlessly mulling over the circumstances of his catastrophic mistake? Probably no longer in the motor-racing business. Or maybe he was able to shrug the whole thing off, as just one of those things that happen? People respond very differently to embarrassment.

Football managers get used to their club's supporters heckling them when the team aren't performing well. But former Aston Villa boss David O'Leary suffered more abuse than most from the fans. O'Leary responded to incessant chanting from the crowd by accusing the supporters of being fickle. At the next home match he looked up into the crowd to see a giant banner declaring: 'We're not fickle. We just don't like you.'

Missing medal

Eighteen-year-old rower Vyacheslav Ivanov was absolutely thrilled with his Olympic gold medal in the single sculls at the 1956 Melbourne Olympics. So thrilled, in fact, that he got carried away when it was presented to him, leapt up and down and managed to drop it into the lake.

Ivanov dived in after it, but to no avail. He was eventually presented with a replacement and went on to win (and hold on to) gold again in the following two Olympic Games.

Good grouping

Cricketer Andrew Symonds hit a ball over the boundary for six runs while playing for Gloucestershire against Sussex in June 1995. The ball struck spectator Paddy Gardner in the face, giving her a black eye. Symonds kept on batting while Paddy was treated with an ice pack. Later in his innings, Symonds struck another six, this time hitting Paddy on the leg. The embarrassed Australian-born batsman bought her flowers at the end of the game.

It's not cricket

Wisden records that the great Yorkshire and England left-arm spinner Bobby Peel was twice found to be playing while seriously under the influence of alcohol. On one occasion he was dropped from the team after beginning his run-up facing the wrong way, bowling in the direction of the pavilion. On another occasion, in 1897, he actually relieved himself on the pitch. He was banished from the field and never played for Yorkshire or England again.

Lost at Lords

The 33-year-old, grey-haired, bespectacled Northamptonshire cricketer David Steele was a surprise selection to play for England against Australia at Lord's in 1975. At the fall of a wicket, it was his turn to make his way out of the pavilion onto the pitch. David had played at Lord's many times but had always been in the visitors' dressing room. Confused, he took a wrong turning, went down several flights of stairs and ended up in the toilets.

The crowd, and the players from both teams, waited patiently until he finally found his way onto the pitch. Described in one newspaper as 'the bank clerk who went to war', Steele went on to become a national hero, with a series of high-scoring batting performances against the formidable pace-bowling of Australia's Dennis Lillee and Jeff Thompson.

And he was voted BBC Sports Personality of the Year. Embarrassment can be survived.

We've nearly all forgotten to turn the clocks backwards or forwards at some time or other, and the consequences can be embarrassing, particularly if we miss an important appointment. In the sports world, getting the time wrong can be disastrous.

Not a morning person

Runner Wim Esajas from Surinam was his country's only representative at the 1960 Olympics in Rome. On the day of his 800m event, Esajas decided to rest at the Olympic Village before going to the track for the afternoon competition. There was one problem; when Esajas arrived, he discovered that the 800m heats had been run in the morning and he had been eliminated for not showing up.

At least he got the right day.

The Russians aren't coming

The Russian shooting team arriving at the 1908 Olympics in London discovered that all the events had been completed several days earlier. They were still using the Julian calendar when most other countries had adopted the Gregorian.

The US athletics team had done the same thing in reverse, arriving twelve days earlier than they intended for the first modern Olympic Games in Greece in 1896. They had been using the Gregorian calendar, while their Greek hosts were using the Julian. Their error didn't prevent the US team from dominating both track and field events.

* * *

One sure way to survive most forms of sporting embarrassment – as competitor, manager, official or commentator – is not to take yourself, or your sport, too seriously. It also helps to adopt the good old British attitude, as personified by Eddie 'The Eagle' Edwards, that it's not the winning but the taking part that's important.

Eddie, you'll remember, became one of the stars of the 1988 Winter Olympics, despite his entirely hopeless efforts in the 90m ski jump. Spectators loved the way the Cheltenham plasterer, after each incompetent jump, raised his arms in triumph, celebrating the fact that yet again he hadn't broken his neck. But never, even when interviewed more than fifteen years later for a TV programme showcasing 'the most embarrassing things about the 80s', did he ever display the slightest hint of embarrassment.

A role model for us all.

CHAPTER NINE

IMPERFECT BODIES

We were walking along Dean Street in London's Soho, on our way home from an evening at the Groucho Club, when accident-prone Martin Plimmer slipped on the banana skin. He went down in a flurry of arms and legs. I struggled to suppress a laugh. Slipping on a banana skin is a comedy cliché, but not something you see every day.

Martin bounced back to his feet and strode on as if nothing had happened. It was more than a week later when I noticed long scars down the backs of both his arms. He'd actually hurt himself quite badly, but had been too embarrassed to admit it.

Our bodies are a great disappointment to us, both in form and function. We can be embarrassed by almost anything about them: height, weight, bottom-size, absence of hair, excess of hair, freckles, noses, ears, breasts and, as several dozen spam emails a day testify, penises. Our bodies wrinkle, pucker and sag in a variety of unfortunate ways. They let us down when we need them to perform – in bed, on the sports field, or doing the watusi. We drop things, spill things, bump into things. And our digestive systems clearly hate us. We are altogether a thoroughly poor piece of design.

Well not you, obviously, but everyone else.

Most of the time we just about come to terms with our inadequacies, real or imagined, and are generally prepared to show our imperfect faces in public. But there are some real dangers lurking here. Poor body image can lead to serious medical conditions, and when embarrassment deters us from visiting the doctor to discuss 'problems with our waterworks' for example, the consequences can be fatal.

We'll come back to that in a moment. In the meantime let's concentrate on some thoroughly humiliating, but non life-threatening conditions ... like flatulence.

It's a gas, gas, gas

Nick Fer was the only man in a Pilates class in a church hall in Clapham in south London. Singled out to demonstrate a particular exercise position, and with twenty pairs of female eyes upon him, he rolled onto his back, brought his knees up to his chest and became (to put it delicately) the victim of a sudden and involuntary explosion of wind – long, loud and exquisitely mortifying. It wasn't Nick's first Pilates class, but it was his last.

Star of musical theatre Michael Ball has been there.

Showstopper

Michael Ball was appearing on stage in Andrew Lloyd Webber's *Aspects of Love*. He had just finished singing a lullaby to the young actress Diana Morrison, who was playing his niece. Into the poignant silence that followed he let rip the most outrageous 'bottom burp'. It could be heard clearly in the gods.

'It totally ruined the entire performance', he says. 'It was awful. The worst moment of my entire career.'

Michael admits that he often gets 'windy' when nervous. Which might have accounted for Julian Clary's failure to control his bodily exhalations while being introduced to the Queen after a Royal Variety Performance. How did Her Majesty respond? She moved rapidly on to Frankie Dettori.

There are products which reduce the risk of such things happening, but buying them in the chemist's can be as embarrassing as asking for something for the weekend, possibly more so.

Psychologists have examined consumer behaviour relating to buying wind and diarrhoea products. Counter-intuitively, it turns out that people who are high in public self-consciousness (HPUBSC) are the most likely to buy them. Studies show that they are prepared to suffer the short-term embarrassment of buying products that would prevent them suffering greater humiliation in the long term. Therefore it was the low in public self-consciousness (LPUBSC) consumers who were the more likely to end up suffering the embarrassment of uncontrolled flatulence and loss of bowel control.

Julian Clary clearly falls into the second category. His spontaneous royal performance was unfortunate, but he wasn't the first to do it.

In bad odour

Edward de Vere, the 17th Earl of Oxford, is believed by some to have been the true author of a number of the plays attributed to William Shakespeare. He was a favourite of Queen Elizabeth I and, it seems, a martyr to his digestive system.

In his *Brief Lives*, the 17th-century biographer John Aubrey recounts the otherwise uncorroborated tale of how the Earl 'while making low obeisance' to her Majesty in court one day, inadvertently 'broke wind'.

De Vere went into voluntary exile. On his return to court, several years later, the Queen's first words to him were: 'My Lord, I had quite forgotten the fart.'

Bill Bryson's body doesn't seem to know what a successful author he has become, and still insists on embarrassing him in public – particularly when he's asleep. In his book about Australia, *Down Under*, Bill describes how he once dropped off while being driven around Sydney by a sales rep from his local publishers. The man, his wife and two young daughters were subjected to an unedifying performance.

I sleep as if injected with a powerful experimental muscle relaxant. My legs fall open in a grotesque come-hither manner; my knuckles brush the floor. Whatever is inside – tongue, uvula, moist bubbles of intestinal air – decides to leak out. From time to time, like one of those nodding-duck toys, my head tips forward to empty a quart or so of viscous drool onto my lap, then falls back to begin loading again with a noise like a toilet cistern filling. And I snore, hugely and helplessly, like a cartoon character, with rubbery flapping lips and prolonged steam-valve exhalations.

It is a terrible burden to bear.

We reflected in the last chapter on the mortification of the long-distance runner, when Paula Radcliffe was caught short in the middle of the London Marathon. Inadequate Bladder Syndrome, can strike anyone, anywhere.

My not so big fat bladder

Actress Nia Vardalos is best known for her starring role in the film *My Big Fat Greek Wedding*.

In her next film, *Connie and Carla*, she had to wear a particularly tight-fitting dress. 'I had to be literally sewn into it', she recalls. Which was fine until halfway through shooting the scene, she needed to answer the call of nature. She approached the assistant director and whispered that she needed to visit the bathroom.

'No problem', he said, picking up a walkie-talkie. 'Nia has to pee', he announced. 'Nia has to pee.'

'You could hear it all across the set', says Nia, 'as I was being walked to my trailer like a zoo animal'.

Premature hair loss ranks high on the list of embarrassing bodily defects, and there are millions of sufferers. Liberal Democrat MP Mark Oaten says his hair loss was the trigger for his midlife crisis and subsequent sex scandal. 'Any television appearance would result in a barrage of emails, not about the issues I'd raised but about my lack of hair', says Oaten. 'It's not surprising that I became more and more obsessed by its disappearance. For me it was a public sign that my youth had ended.'

Baldness strikes indiscriminately, regardless of wealth, status or political persuasion. It struck Adnan Kashoggi, Lenin, Elton John, Silvio Berlusconi, Homer Simpson, Prince Charles and, indeed, Queen Elizabeth I. Though none of these, unlike Oaten, used it to excuse an affair with a rent boy.

Cutting a rug

US television host Ed Sullivan once let slip that actor George Burns wore a toupee. Furious, Burns remonstrated with Sullivan for revealing his embarrassing secret.

'But, George', Sullivan said, 'I didn't think you'd mind'.

'If I didn't mind', Burns replied, 'why would I wear a toupee?'

Those embarrassed by hair loss have recourse to toupees, transplants and titfers. Obesity is harder to cover up.

Incredible shrinking man

City banker Tom Armour was a very, very big man.

At his largest, his neck measurement was 23 inches and he was five feet around the waist. His weight fluctuated between 26 and 30 stone. Not, ladies and gentlemen, the fattest man in the world, but in the ballpark. For years Tom had been too embarrassed to go to weddings or parties, and was often insulted in the street. He was miserable, but still he did nothing about it.

And yet by July 2006, after eighteen months on a tough regime of diet and exercise, he had reduced his weight to under fourteen stone, and become Slimming World's 'man of the year'.

It was his fourteen-year-old daughter Lorna who had shamed him into action. He'd gone to pick her up from a party, a task which usually fell to his wife. Lorna got into his car in tears, saying: 'Why did you come? Now my friends know what you look like.'

It was an embarrassment too far for Tom, who began dieting the very next day.

If we run out of physiological things to become embarrassed about, we can always fall back on our phobias. Some, of course, are seriously debilitating, but many are just plain humiliating. My fear of moths has, as I have mentioned, made me a laughing stock on many occasions. A friend is terrified of buttons, particularly those loosely attached to clothing.

Some people, I've learned, are scared of long words. It's called hippopotomonstrosesquippedaliophobia, which presumably prevents sufferers from telling anybody what they've got.

There is, pretty much, a phobia for everything. I've never met anyone suffering from alektorophobia, but I know not to bother looking for them around chickens. I have no interest at all in those who suffer from bibliophobia – a fear of books. However, this book should be of particular interest to those afflicted by ereuthrophobia, fear of blushing, and catagelophobia, fear of being ridiculed. And as a lifelong devourer of peanut butter, my heart goes out to those suffering from arachibutyrophobia, who are scared of getting the stuff stuck to the roofs of their mouths. I'm not making these up.

But for all of you out there, embarrassed by your unmentionable or unpronounceable phobias, there is hope.

Getting to the root of the problem

Krissie Palmer-Howart suffered for more than 40 years from lachanophobia – a fear of vegetables. The 61-year-old cabaret singer from Newhaven in East Sussex was not only unable to handle vegetables, she couldn't even say their names. Their smell made her sick.

But after undergoing hypnotherapy, Miss Palmer-Howarth says she can now tolerate being close to vegetables, even broccoli which she detests most of all. She has not yet, however, reached the stage where she can cuddle a cabbage, let alone actually eat a vegetable.

Miss Palmer-Howarth puts her condition down to the awful smells in her uncle's greengrocer's shop when she was a child. 'It's a stupid thing to be scared of', she admits.

It's lucky she doesn't also suffer from hypnophobia. Actually I did invent that one – I think.

* * *

Our species has adapted inadequately to life on two legs. It's a constant source of surprise that department stores still insist on piling glassware and bone china within easy striking range of our poorly controlled elbows and knees. The proverbial bull might do less damage. And if there's anything worse than accidentally smashing an expensive figurine to smithereens, it's seeing someone else do it. Vicarious embarrassment can be worse than the self-inflicted kind. The clumsy culprit can at least apologise or pay for any damage he or she has done. The embarrassed onlooker is helpless.

Would you rather have watched Nick Flynn's behaviour – or have been Nick Flynn?

Gone to pot

Nick Flynn said it was a 'regrettable accident' when, in February 2006, he tripped on his shoelaces and fell down stairs at the Fitzwilliam Museum in Cambridge, shattering three 300-year-old Qing vases.

Variously valued at between £75,000 and £500,000, the vases were among the best-known exhibits at the museum, where they had stood on a recessed window-sill since 1948. They were not insured.

'I snagged my shoelace, missed a step and crash, bang, wallop and there was a million pieces of high-quality Qing ceramics lying around underneath me', said 42-year-old Mr Flynn. 'I think the management are a bit embarrassed at the moment, with them being worth such a considerable amount.'

The museum director wrote to Mr Flynn, a regular visitor, asking him not to visit again 'in the near future'.

Nick Flynn seems to have been the person least embarrassed by what he described as his 'Norman Wisdom moment', taking the view that the museum should have placed the vases in a more secure place, or at least provided a hand rail on the staircase. If you can prove it's not your fault, it's slightly less embarrassing.

Multimillionaire casino owner Steve Wynn couldn't deny culpability for his own piece of art vandalism, committed in October 2006.

Giving Picasso the elbow

With one expansive wave of his arm, US casino mogul Steve Wynn wiped millions from the value of his Picasso painting. It was an expensive and hugely embarrassing bit of clumsiness.

He was showing his £74 million picture *Le Rêve* (The Dream) to guests at his office in Las Vegas when he accidentally struck it with his right elbow, tearing a small hole in the canvas. Mr Wynn, who has retinitis pigmentosa, an eye disease affecting peripheral vision, had to call off his planned sale of the painting, which he'd bought in 1997 for $48.4 million.

'Look what I've done', he said at the time. Adding, as only a multimillionaire could: 'Thank goodness it was me.'

* * *

When your body lets you down in a sporting arena, there's nowhere to hide.

In the diving events at the Olympics, for example, ungainly and painful-looking collisions between springboards and heads are not uncommon. The great US Olympic champion Greg Louganis received two black eyes and a bloody nose after hitting a platform in 1976, was knocked unconscious in 1979, and broke a collarbone in 1981. Divers must practise their three-and-a-half somersault tucks a thousand times, so why don't they know where the board is?

And then there are goalkeepers.

You make me want to shout

In 1975, Manchester United keeper Alex Stepney somehow managed to dislocate his jaw while shouting at his defenders during a game against Birmingham City.

Not a goalkeeper's best friend

Brentford goalie Chic Brodie had his career brought to an untimely end by a dog. During a game against Colchester United in November 1970, a black-and-white terrier invaded the pitch and ran straight towards Brodie, just as he was bending down to retrieve a back pass. The ensuing collision sent the keeper crashing to the ground, shattering his kneecap. Brodie was stretchered off in agony and never played professional football again.

Embarrassing accidents can prevent sportspeople from competing in the first place. It was a dog which extended Belgian tennis star Kim Clijsters' list of career-threatening injuries when she tripped over her own pooch while playing football and bruised her coccyx. This is an embarrassing injury, however you get it.

He's a pink toothbrush

In 1906, US tennis champion Beals C. Wright was trying to recover from a hangover ahead of a crucial Davis Cup competition. He rang room service and ordered a bottle of soda water. It arrived without a bottle opener, so Beals rather unwisely tried to open it using a toothbrush.

The bottle broke at the neck and gashed his right hand. An infection set in and he was rushed to hospital for a life-saving operation. He survived, but one of his fingers had to be amputated.

Poke at a pig

The Cook Islands weightlifter Mike Tereui ruined his chances of taking part in the 1990 Commonwealth Games by breaking a hand throwing a punch at a pig which raided his vegetable patch.

And yet another goalkeeper.

Freak control accident

England and Arsenal goalkeeper David Seaman missed the first half of the 1996–97 season after damaging his knee ligaments bending down to pick up his television remote control.

And so near, yet so far.

Hamstrung

In an American football game against the St Louis Rams in 1981, Baltimore Colts offensive guard Robert Pratt pulled a hamstring – while running onto the field for the pre-game warm-up.

Dying of embarrassment

Our bodies can make us look complete fools when they let us down, but we usually survive the experience. However, our failure to acknowledge the limitations of our physical frailty can have more serious, even potentially fatal, consequences.

My eyes started to grow dim around the age of nine or ten, but I denied my ophthalmologic handicap for an absurdly long time, not wanting to join the other 'four-eyes' in the playground. I was probably eleven when I eventually gave in to the inevitable and allowed my father to take me to see the optician. I remember the man shining a little torch into my eye. Looking up into his face and seeing his nostril hairs, I dissolved in a fit of hysterics and had to be taken out and walked up and down the street until I calmed down. I was eventually supplied with a pair of ghastly NHS glasses, which were no laughing matter.

Well into my teens, I was still avoiding wearing my specs unless it was absolutely essential, worrying that they signalled some sort of inadequacy. Interviewed for a job as a grocery delivery boy, I hid my glasses for fear they would prejudice my chances of employment, and had to spend the next couple of years cycling away from the shop, into heavy traffic, in a myopic blur. It was a miracle I didn't kill myself.

Embarrassment can lead us to risk death in a variety of ways. I've heard of a fisherman who almost drowned after falling in a canal, because he was too embarrassed to call for help. And a psychological study back in 1979 reported cases of excessively reserved people who were actually prepared to quietly choke to death in a restaurant rather than draw attention to themselves.

There's a range of medical conditions we're reluctant to discuss, even with our GP, including athlete's foot, impotence, incontinence and memory loss. More worryingly, we display similar reticence about admitting symptoms of more life-threatening ailments such as sexually transmitted diseases. Former Ugandan president Idi Amin once ordered that venereal disease should be renamed 'good hope' so that sufferers wouldn't be too embarrassed to visit a clinic. And colon cancer claims thousands of lives every year, largely because people are too embarrassed to discuss the symptoms with their doctor.

* * *

Not only can we die as a result of embarrassment, we can also die (or at least do ourselves serious mischief) in extremely embarrassing ways. 'Asphyxiated during autoerotic sex-play' is not what I want to see (and am very unlikely to see) at the bottom of my *Times* obituary.

Sometimes we escape our semi-suicidal stupidity with just some embarrassing scars.

There goes a whizzbang

A British squaddie, just back from a tour of duty in Iraq, decided to entertain his friends during the November 5th bonfire night celebrations in Sunderland by imitating a stunt from the film *Jackass: The Movie*. Twenty-two-year-old Andrew Tilley dropped his trousers, lay on his stomach, carefully placed a Black Cat Thunderbolt rocket in his bottom, then instructed a friend to light the blue touch paper and retire ...

Bleeding profusely from his backside, Tilley was rushed to hospital to be treated for a scorched colon. An emergency service spokesman said the young man's behaviour definitely contravened the Firework Safety Code.

Accident and Emergency departments are quite used to people coming in asking to have things removed from their rectums. Among the objects reported to have been extracted are carrots, turnips and various types of fruit, a mobile phone, a snuff box, a toothbrush, a hard-boiled egg, a frozen pig's tail and a pepper pot inscribed 'A present from Margate'.

The case of a twenty-year-old klismaphiliac (someone with an enema fetish) was written up in the *American Journal of Forensic Medicine and Pathology*. The young man was treated for 'an impacted foreign body in his rectum following an enema with a concrete mix'. The all too solid object was removed, and the patient kept in hospital overnight for observation. He left in the morning, declining offers of psychiatric help.

In 1994, Californian molecular biologist Wendy Northcutt started a website dedicated to recording the Darwin Awards – spoof tributes to those who 'improve the human genome by accidentally killing themselves in really stupid ways'.

Just a couple of her award-winners:

A clean way to go

In May 2004, police in Wolfsberg, Austria, were called to an apartment house where they found the body of a man, his legs dangling out of a ground-floor window. Entering the building, they discovered the deceased's head soaking in a sink full of hot water.

It transpired that the man had arrived home late at night, high on drink and drugs, and attempted to climb in through the kitchen window. The window was fixed at the base and tilted out, enabling him to squeeze through until his head reached the sink, whereupon he got stuck. Struggling to free himself, he managed to turn on the hot water tap.

Police couldn't account for why he hadn't simply turned off the water, pulled out the plug or, even more simply, entered through the front door in the first place. They found his house keys in his trouser pocket.

The fastest man in the cemetery

The fastest human beings can achieve a maximum sprint speed of around 16mph, and can't keep that up for long.

Unfortunately this vital piece of information escaped a nineteen-year-old Dutch motorist who chose a bizarre way to impress his friends. Driving along the A67 highway near the town of Blerick, he put his car on cruise control at 20mph and stepped out of the vehicle. His intention was to briefly run alongside the car, then jump back in, but the second his feet hit the ground he slammed head-first into the road. He was rushed to hospital with severe brain damage, and died the next day.

Death does not always become us.

* * *

No one's perfect, and we needn't be embarrassed about that. Better that we acknowledge, even celebrate, our imperfections and foibles and weaknesses. They are, after all, what make each of us unique.

Just two pieces of advice.

1) The doctor has heard it all before.
2) Don't eat Jerusalem artichokes before a Pilates class. (And never admit a fart. American writer Paul Auster, in his novel

The Brooklyn Follies, tells the cautionary tale of eleven-year-old Dudley Franklin who broke wind in a geography class, blushed ruby red and mumbled 'excuse me'. He was forever after known as Excuse-Me Franklin.)

Oh yes, and don't stick a firework up your arse.

CHAPTER TEN

HOW TO BEAT EMBARRASSMENT

Embarrassment, as we've seen, can cause us a lot of grief. It holds us back in life, controls the way we behave, wrecks careers and can even kill.

But embarrassment is not without its redeeming qualities. A world in which no one was ever remotely embarrassed would be unbearable, full of men and women behaving badly, doing as they damn well pleased, trampling all over each other's feelings without a hint of remorse.

Embarrassment is fine and dandy in its place, policing our inappropriate or antisocial behaviour. The trouble is that it so often behaves like 'Bad Cop', exceeding its authority, beating us up in the cells with its big fat truncheon.

I have, for example, spent more than 30 years regretting my part in a rather juvenile prank. I'd been drinking with friends in a country pub and we were driving home in two cars. Those of us in the leading vehicle suddenly decided it would be hilariously funny to pretend we had crashed. Our driver, and the ringleader in the escapade, swerved off the road and nudged the car gently against a tree. We then draped ourselves lifelessly out of doors and windows, and waited. Arriving at the scene, our friends rushed over to us and we all leapt up, laughing uproariously. They were not amused. In fact they were furious, particularly my old college flatmate Dennis, who considered our actions to have been 'fucking immature'.

Dennis and I never mentioned the matter again and some years later he moved to Barcelona and we lost touch. Back in contact now, and having decided to write about the incident, I asked him what he remembered about it. I had always assumed that he remained as cross about it as I remained ashamed. He replied, of course, that he only 'dimly, dimly' recalled it happening, was amazed at my capacity for remembering such events, and certainly harboured no ill-feelings. I'd suffered 30 unnecessary years of embarrassment-fuelled remorse.

OK, if I'd been more easily embarrassed in the first place, I might never have got involved in such stupid behaviour, but my protracted feelings of guilt were completely out of proportion to the crime. Embarrassment punishes us excessively for our indiscretions. Embarrassment is an emotional bully, but it can, I think, be cowed.

It can certainly be avoided, though this may involve severe restrictions on our freedom of movement. In my case it would require the avoidance of moths, bacon-slicers, broom cupboards and, to be honest, almost any situation where my memory, physical skills or judgement might be put to the test.

That's me. For those made of sterner stuff, there's still a list of embarrassment black spots to be avoided. These would certainly include haemorrhoids, dating, sex, parties, golf clothes, sport in general, work, pantomimes, Pilates and Sacha Baron Cohen.

We are ticking embarrassment time bombs just waiting to explode in our own and each other's faces. We need help from the embarrassment bomb squad.

The cure

The first step towards defusing embarrassment is to accept that our typical reaction to our own faux pas is almost always out of proportion to the events which generated it.

Extreme responses to embarrassment can result in serious social phobia – an overwhelming need to hide from the world. More commonly, however, they manifest themselves as shyness. Shyness is defined by Dr Lynne Henderson of California's Shyness Clinic as 'a shrinking back from life. A weakening of the bonds of human connection.' As with social anxiety and social phobia, it's based, she says, on 'faulty patterns of perception, irrational beliefs, and excessively high performance standards'.

In other words, we expect too much from ourselves, and are prone to view our behaviour in an unnecessarily poor light. Fortunately there are people who can help us mend our ways.

Psychotherapist Linda Crawford, director of the London Shyness Centre, can make you brim with confidence. She offers biomagnetism, neuro-linguistic programming and hypnotism among her treatments. And psychologists have a range of 'cognitive interventions' to address anything from shyness to full-blown social phobia. These include 'Rational-Emotive Therapy', which helps patients recognise the unrealistic and self-defeating nature of their thoughts, as well as 'Systematic Rational Restructuring' and 'Self-control Desensitisation', which both involve practical training in how to handle difficult social situations.

And it's all completely painless.

Or you could try something a little more self-help orientated. Writer Fiona J. Bowron has produced an amusing and highly instructive little book called *1001 Ways to Humiliate Yourself and Others (to Cause Embarrassment Wherever You Go)*. She adheres to the school of thought that humiliation can actually be a good thing; though it's not, she concedes, a very large school, and probably not one that you'd fight to have your children attend.

The theory is that our need for self-esteem gets in the way of true enlightenment. By embracing total humiliation we can overcome our need for self-esteem, and become enlightened. Once enlightened, Fiona suggests, we will no longer suffer humiliation and embarrassment.

The book's 90 or so pages of advice on how to embrace humiliation can really be boiled down to two key suggestions.

- Make a habit of being inept.
- Always be on the lookout for new things you can fail at.

* * *

Blushing is one of the most obvious indications of embarrassment, but it's also a major cause. Blushing draws attention to our embarrassment, which causes us further embarrassment, and so on. It's a vicious circle in scarlet. But here too there is help at hand.

At the extreme end there's surgery – endoscopic transthoracic sympathectomy. The procedure involves interrupting the sympathetic nerve pathway to the face, effectively destroying the neural circuitry that controls blushing. Alas, it has some rather unfortunate side effects, including profuse sweating, which can be, of course, rather embarrassing.

Psychologist Robert Edelmann has devoted much of his career to studying embarrassment, and has been consulted by many people whose lives have been blighted by blushing. These include nurses, teachers, accountants, even one 31-year-old barrister from Norwich who has never appeared in court since qualifying, fearing that her profuse blushing would stop people taking her seriously.

Professor Edelmann's book *Coping with Blushing* offers a variety of strategies including muscle-control exercises to create relaxation and improve breathing. It advises on re-evaluating and redirecting thoughts to eliminate negative thinking, and offers a number of 'distraction techniques'. The underlying message is that sufferers need to become less concerned with their own behaviour and others' reactions. Applying his techniques, he claims, should alleviate blushing and make life a lot less embarrassing all round.

* * *

Comedy writer and actor Ricky Gervais understands embarrassment. He's made a very lucrative career out of it.

> The worst thing in the world is a social faux pas – being embarrassed. I can sort of hand it out but I can't take it. If I watch something on television, a reality game show, and someone's being pretentious or flirting or talking about themselves in the third person, it's embarrassing. So I know what I don't like, and I try and put that into comedy.

And he has some useful advice for people who find themselves in embarrassing situations.

> I feel for them. If someone goes to the toilet and they come out and there's a big wet part, but no one says anything, then they discover it, how embarrassing is that? But what if you come out and say, 'Look, I pissed myself'. Right? It's not embarrassing.

Not everyone will be comfortable with admitting they flunked toilet-training class. Better, perhaps, to have a range of excuses up your sleeve, ready for a whole range of embarrassing circumstances. The following can be applied, as appropriate.

- It wasn't me.
- I didn't mean it.
- Tummy trouble.
- It was the dog.
- A little bit too much to drink.
- Not feeling very well.
- Suffering from amnesia/stress/anxiety.
- I've been brainwashed/hypnotised.
- I had to do it. They're holding my wife at gunpoint.

If all your excuses are rejected, try losing your temper. The literary critic Professor Christopher Ricks studied embarrassment, and argued that the best antidote is to get your retaliation in first.

> Indignation stands interestingly to embarrassment; the one hot flush drives out the other, as fire fire, so that a common way of staving off embarrassment one would otherwise feel is by inciting oneself to indignation.

A practical application would be: 'Well I may have smashed your priceless Chinese vase, but it's your own stupid fault for placing it within one mile of me in the first place.'

But what are you to do if a confession is totally inappropriate, no excuse seems adequate, and losing your temper would just make things worse? Dustin Hoffman has the solution.

On your toes

Barry Levinson's 1997 film *Wag the Dog* was a political satire about a phoney war invented by spin doctors to

223

draw attention away from a president's sexual impropriety.

Months later came the real-life revelations about a sex scandal involving President Clinton and Monica Lewinsky, followed by US military action in the Balkans and the Middle East. Some suggested it was almost as if the film-makers had seen into the future.

Shortly afterwards, Levinson and the stars of the film, Dustin Hoffman and Robert De Niro, happened to meet Clinton at a reception. Clinton asked De Niro what their most recent film was about.

Acutely embarrassed, De Niro just looked at Levinson; Levinson looked at Hoffman; Hoffman, unable to think of anything to say, resorted to extreme measures. He started to tap dance.

And if you can't tap dance? In the final analysis, there's one sure-fire way to combat embarrassment. In even the most humiliating of situations, we must, at all costs, maintain a sense of humour.

Embarrassment akimbo

The American columnist and author Franklin Pierce Adams once accompanied Beatrice Kaufman, the wife of playwright George S. Kaufman, to a cocktail party.

Feeling a little light-headed, Beatrice sat down on a cane chair – which promptly collapsed, leaving her trapped in the frame, her legs splayed in the air.

Breaking the shocked silence that greeted the performance, Adams turned to his companion and said, entirely straight-faced: 'I've told you a hundred times, Beatrice ... that's not funny.'

History doesn't record whether or not poor Mrs K. found it funny.

One giant false step for man

Embarrassment, as we've seen, can place a permanent stain on our record, blotting out our achievements in life. But science can, on rare occasions, turn things around.

Astronaut Neil Armstrong's pleasure in becoming the first man on the Moon was somewhat tarnished by his embarrassment at committing one of the great verbal gaffes of the 20th century.

Climbing down from the lunar module, Armstrong had planned to say: 'That's one small step for a man, one giant leap for mankind.' But to all the world – and just about all the world was listening – he seemed to miss out the 'a', delivering the tautological and rather meaningless: '... one small step for man, one giant leap for mankind.' Had he fluffed his lines, or had the word 'a' been drowned out by static? Even Armstrong admitted he wasn't sure, commenting: 'Damn, I really did it. I blew the first words on the Moon, didn't I?'

But in October 2006 a recording of Armstrong's words was put through sophisticated new computer software which conclusively established that an incredibly faint acoustic soundwave from the word 'a' was, in fact, there. Neil Armstrong can now sleep easily in his bed knowing that he won't go down in history as the man who made the first faux pas on the Moon.

Alas, science can do little to help Michael Ball or George Bush Snr, or you and me. It can't remove the embarrassment associated with breaking wind on the West End stage or vomiting in the lap of the Japanese Prime Minister, or most of the misadventures which bedevil all our lives. Science can't (yet) make it possible for us to retrieve our misdirected or regretted emails after we have pressed SEND. Science can't enable us to lead our lives 'in delay', like a *Big Brother* transmission, so that we can erase our gaffes before they go public. Until such things are possible, we're on our own, in sole control of our own embarrassing futures.

Good luck.

SOURCES OF EMBARRASSMENT

David Allyn, *I Can't Believe I Just Did That*, Tarcher Penguin, 2004

Fiona J. Bowron, *1001 Ways to Humiliate Yourself and Others*, New Holland, 2004

Bill Bryson, *Down Under*, Doubleday, 2000

Bill Bryson, *The Life and Times of the Thunderbolt Kid*, Doubleday, 2006

Michael Bywater, *Big Babies*, Granta, 2006

Frances Coverdale and Clare Price, *Red Face Stories*, Two Covers, 2006

Robert Drennen, *The Algonquin Wits*, Replica Books, 2000

Robert J. Edelmann, *The Psychology of Embarrassment*, John Wiley, 1987

Robert J. Edelmann, *Coping with Blushing*, Sheldon Press, 2004

Norbert Elias, *The Civilizing Process*, Blackwell Publishing, 2000

Cordelia Fine, *A Mind of its Own*, Icon Books, 2005

Kate Fox, *Watching the English*, Hodder, 2005

Cris Freddi, *The Guinness Book of Sporting Blunders*, Guinness, 1996

Ian Gittins, *Weddings From Hell*, Granada, 1998

M. Hirsh Goldberg, *The Blunder Book*, Quill, 1984

Barbara G. Markway, *Dying of Embarrassment*, New Harbinger Publications, 1992

Rowland S. Miller, *Embarrassment*, The Guilford Press, 1996

Robert Morley, *Book of Bricks*, Weidenfeld and Nicolson, 1978

Margaret Moser, *Movie Stars Do the Dumbest Things*, Renaissance Books, 1999

Philip Norman, *Awful Moments*, Penguin, 1986

Simon Pearce, *That Which is Not Said*, Look At You Productions, 2006

Stephen Pile, *The Book of Heroic Failures*, Secker & Warburg, 1979

Stephen Pile, *The Return of Heroic Failures*, Secker & Warburg, 1988

Martin Plimmer, *King of the Castle*, Ebury Press, 2002

Ronald Reagan, *An American Life*, Pocket Books, 1999

Christopher Ricks, *Keats and Embarrassment*, OUP, 1976

Robin Robertson (ed.), *Mortification*, Harper Perennial, 2004

Katherine Ann Samon, *Dates from Hell*, Plume, 1992

Fiona Snelson (ed.), *The NSPCC Book of Famous Faux Pas*, Century, 1990

Ivan Ward and Oscar Zarate, *Introducing Psychoanalysis*, Icon Books, 2002

I Hate the Office

Malcolm Burgess

A dark, edgy, yet laugh-out-loud A to Z of the absurdities and horrors of corporate life, from the pages of London's *Metro* newspaper.

Who, when they were six years old, ever said, 'Hey, I want to spend forty years of my life wondering what value-added knowledge capital is in a size-restricted cubicle surrounded by people who watch *Bargain Hunt*'?

500 Reasons Why...

I Hate The Office

Malcolm Burgess

Office workers of the world unite!

What makes the 9.00-to-5.30 sentence quite so gruesome? Office escapee Malcolm Burgess offers a painfully hilarious A to Z of reasons why the office has become the modern byword for servitude.

From the agony of the Away Day via hot desking, office politics, romances and parties, to the sheer terror of work reunions or conference calls, Burgess vents his spleen on the working week.

Ending with the unique Corporate Bullshit Detector, *I Hate the Office* is every stressed-out worker's essential weapon in the war against the angst of modern office life.

Hardback £9.99

ISBN 10: 1-84046-779-7   ISBN 13: 978-1840467-79-6

Forty-fied

The Good, the Bad and the Sad of Fortysomething Life

Malcolm Burgess

Is being forty the new thirty or are we all just kidding ourselves?

Malcolm Burgess presents a riotous A to Z of the realities of fortysomething life in the Noughties. Riotous, that is, like having your iPod on in the house. Today's fortysomethings have never had it so good – or so confusing. While our parents could look forward to a sensible middle age we're more likely to be playing our Morrissey records and thanking God Jonathan Ross is on Radio 2. There are so many different ways of being in our forties that many of us aren't quite sure where we're supposed to go next – or just how grumpy we're meant to be.

Forty-fied is the hilariously wry and observant essential guide to this complex decade in our lives. The *Metro* columnist and bestselling author of *I Hate the Office* leaves no embarrassing fortysomething scenario unturned – or do we mean unstoned?

For anyone forty and fabulous, or who's forty and owns ten fleeces, this is the laugh-out-loud funny book of your dreams … and no doubt your screams, too.

Hardback £9.99

Published in September 2007

ISBN 10: 1-84046-823-8   ISBN 13: 978-1840468-23-6

The Lying Ape

An Honest Guide to a World of Deception

Brian King

Brian King reveals our all-embracing culture of lies and deception in this brilliant exposé of the duplicity of modern life. We are all liars, telling an average of six per day. So the next time you speak to someone, the chances are that you will be lied to. Or that you will lie.

The Lying Ape unravels the full extent of the deceit that surrounds us. King explores the deceptions of obvious candidates such as politicians, ad-men, journalists and secondhand car salesmen, as well as the subtler falsehoods of our partners and children, including the white lies we all tell each other to preserve our precious self-esteem.

He also looks at the great liars of history, reveals how scientists can observe the brain as it suppresses the awkward truth, and advises on the best techniques for spotting a lie through body language and verbal slips.

Essential reading for anyone who's ever tried to live a slightly more honest life …

Paperback £7.99

ISBN 10: 1-84046-799-1   ISBN 13: 978-1840467-99-4

Beyond Coincidence

Stories of amazing
coincidences and the
mystery and mathematics
that lie behind them

*Martin Plimmer and
Brian King*

Laura Buxton, aged ten, releases
a balloon from her garden in
Staffordshire. It lands 140 miles
away in Wiltshire, in the garden of
another Laura Buxton, aged ten.

Coincidence? Or something more?
This remarkable bestseller is a
celebration of the Universe's most
beguiling phenomenon, containing
250 amazing stories of coincidence and many intriguing insights into its
workings.

Often awed but nonetheless gently sceptical, Plimmer and King's book,
developed from the BBC Radio 4 series of the same name, is witty and
consistently amazing.

'Extraordinary stories' *Daily Mail*

'An intriguing investigation of the cosmos's most improbable events …
a first-rate book' *Observer*

'An entertaining and intelligent study' *Mail on Sunday*

'Amazing' Simon Hoggart, *Guardian*

'*Beyond Coincidence* has already resulted in many an overlong stay in
the toilet' David Baddiel

'Hundreds of great stories to keep you entertained' *Focus*

'Guaranteed to send a shiver down your spine' *Good Book Guide*

Paperback £6.99

ISBN 10: 1-84046-618-9   ISBN 13: 978-1840466-18-8